ANGELS
AND
WONDERS

Other Loyola Press Books by Joan Wester Anderson:

GUARDIAN ANGELS:
TRUE STORIES OF ANSWERED PRAYERS

IN THE ARMS OF ANGELS:
TRUE STORIES OF HEAVENLY GUARDIANS

THE POWER OF MIRACLES:
TRUE STORIES OF GOD'S PRESENCE

JOAN WESTER ANDERSON

ANGELS AND WONDERS

TRUE STORIES OF HEAVEN ON EARTH

LOYOLAPRESS.
A JESUIT MINISTRY
Chicago

LOYOLAPRESS.
A JESUIT MINISTRY

3441 N. Ashland Avenue
Chicago, Illinois 60657
(800) 621-1008
www.loyolapress.com

A previous edition of this book was published as *Where Wonders Prevail: True Accounts That Bear Witness to the Existence of Heaven* (New York: Ballantine Books, 1996).

Cover photograph: John H. Burkey
Cover design by Becca Gay
Interior design by Adam Moroschan

Library of Congress Cataloging-in-Publication Data
Anderson, Joan Wester
  Angels and wonders : true stories of heaven on earth / Joan Wester Anderson.
      p. cm.
  Originally published: New York : Ballantine Books, 1996.
  Includes bibliographical references.
  ISBN-13: 978-0-8294-2733-2
  ISBN-10: 0-8294-2733-3
  1. Miracles. I. Title.
  BT97.3.A53 2008
  202'.11—dc22

                                                    2008016433

Printed in the United States of America
14 15 16 17 18 19 20 Versa 10 9 8 7 6 5 4 3 2

To my husband,
with thanks for his encouragement, comfort, and support
throughout my writing career

For I dipped into the future, far as human eye could see,
Saw the vision of the world, and all the wonder that would be.

—ALFRED, LORD TENNYSON, "LOCKSLEY HALL"

CONTENTS

Acknowledgments   **xi**

Prologue   **xiii**

Introduction   **xvii**

For Love of Logan   **1**

Miracle in Mobile   **11**

Invisible Guardians   **17**

Surprise Witness   **21**

Messenger from Cork   **27**

What Do the Children Know?   **35**

God Knows Where We Are   **43**

Dream Maker   **49**

Erin's Christmas Vision   **55**

Heavenly Sights   **63**

Nothing at All Too Small   **73**

With Love, from Above   **77**

Promise on Page One   **85**

Silent Partner   **93**

Bending the Rules   **97**

Vision of Hope   109

Rescue in Nashville   113

Angel Unaware   123

Plenty to Go Around   127

Stranger in the Fire   141

Mary's Mantle   147

The Man in the Photograph   155

Love, from Mother   161

The God Squad   167

Who Wondrous Things Hath Done . . .   173

Marvelous Message   179

Janet's Vision   185

Angelic Lifeguard   193

Love in the Light   197

Canine Sentries   203

Always a Father   209

When We Ask   213

Miracle Man   225

Those Who Wait upon the Lord   231

Wonder at the Well   237

Together at Last   241

Guardians in the Jungle   247

Triumph in the Sky   253

Contents

Epilogue **261**

Notes **263**

Bibliography and Resources **265**

Author's Afterword **269**

About the Author **270**

ACKNOWLEDGMENTS

Many people contribute to the writing of a book. I would like to thank those who took the time to contact me with promising story leads. They include Mary Lou Douglas of Pinson, Alabama; Louise Eldridge of Bangor, Maine; Louise Bergstrom of Dunedin, Florida; Mary Spence Tryba of Riverside, Illinois; Larry Wilhelm of the Full Gospel Businessmen's Association in Dayton, Ohio; Lynn Grisard Fullman of Birmingham, Alabama, author of *Alabama Miracles*; the news department of WTVF-TV in Nashville, Tennessee; and Norman Laster, host of *Dialogue* on radio station WFDU in Fairlawn, New Jersey.

I'm grateful for the technical and professional assistance given to me by George Gallup III, of the Princeton Religion Research Center, Princeton, New Jersey; William P. Kuhn, MD, pediatrician, Arlington Heights, Illinois; Mark Seiderman of the National Climatic Data Center, Asheville, North Carolina; Peter J. Kreeft, professor of philosophy at Boston College, Boston, Massachusetts; Mother Angelica of the Eternal Word Television Network, Birmingham, Alabama; and Barry L. Paschal, editorial writer and former reporter for the *Augusta Chronicle*, Augusta, Georgia. Personnel at *Guideposts* magazine, the Christian Broadcasting Network, the Asher Library at Spertus College of Judaica, the Utah Power and Light Company, and the Centers for Disease Control and Prevention were also helpful, as were fellow authors Chuck Schiappacasse and John Ronner, who, as always, generously shared results of their research.

Perhaps most special are my readers, who phone radio and television talk shows, meet me at signings and lectures, use my books in classes and ministries, write affirming notes, and, in many dear ways, encourage me to continue researching and sharing these stories.

May our eyes always be open to the wonders he sends.

PROLOGUE

Faith, like good poetry, starts with a lump in the throat.

—ROBERT FROST

It was an autumn morning in 1971, shortly after our family moved into our first house. The children were upstairs unpacking containers, and I was looking out the window at my father, moving around mysteriously on the front lawn. My parents lived nearby, and Dad had visited us several times already. "What are you doing out there?" I called to him.

He looked up, smiling. "I'm making you a surprise."

What kind of a surprise? I wondered. Knowing my father, an engaging and quixotic man, it could be just about anything. But Dad would say no more, and caught up in the busyness of our new life, I eventually forgot about it.

Until one raw day in late March when, again, I glanced out the window. Dismal. Overcast. Little piles of dirty snow still stubbornly littering the lawn, as boots and wet mittens cluttered our closets. I had always hated winter—would it *ever* end?

And yet—was it a mirage? I strained to see what I thought was something pink, miraculously peeking out of a drift. And was that a dot of blue across the yard, a small note of optimism in this gloomy expanse? I grabbed my coat and headed outside for a closer look.

They were crocuses, not neatly marching along the house's foundation in typical garden fashion (where I never could have seen them from the window) but scattered whimsically throughout the front lawn. Lavender, blue, yellow, and my favorite pink—little faces bobbing in the bitter wind—they heralded the hope I'd almost lost. "See?" they seemed to say. "You've survived the long dark winter. And if you hang on a little longer, life will be beautiful again."

Dad. I smiled, remembering the bulbs he had secretly planted last fall. What could have been more perfectly timed, more tuned to my needs? How blessed I was, not only for the flowers, but also for him.

My father's crocuses bloomed each spring for the next four or five seasons, bringing that same assurance every time they arrived. *Hard times almost over, light coming, hold on, hold on.* Then, apparently, the bulbs could produce no more. A spring came with only half the usual blooms. The next spring, about 1979, there were none. I missed the crocuses, but my life was busier than ever, and I had never been much of a gardener. *I will ask Dad to come over and plant new bulbs,* I thought. But I never did.

Our father died suddenly, on one exquisitely beautiful day in October 1985. We grieved intensely, deeply, but cleanly, because there was no unfinished business, no regrets or lingering guilt. We had always been a faith-filled family, and we leaned on it now. Of course, Dad was in heaven. Where else would such a beloved person go? He was still a part of us; in fact, he could probably do even more for his family now that he was closer to God.

And if I wondered, just a little, in the quiet darkness of my room, if I unwillingly questioned what I had been taught because faith suddenly seemed to demand more bravery than I could muster, if I silently echoed the words of that long-ago centurion, "I *do* believe! Help my unbelief!" no one else ever knew. We suffered. We handled our pain. We laughed and cried together. Life went on.

Four years passed, and on a dismal day in spring 1989, I found myself running errands and feeling depressed. *Winter blahs,* I told myself. *You get them every year. It's chemistry.* Perhaps. But it was something else, too. Once again I found myself thinking about my father. This was not unusual—we often talked about him, reminiscing and enjoying our memories. But now, in the car, my old concern surfaced. How was he? And, although I hated to wonder, *where* was he? *I know that I know that I know,* I told God in the familiar shorthand I often use. *But do you think you could send a sign, just something little, that Dad is home safe with you?*

Immediately I felt guilty. God had been very good to me, and he had a right to expect something in return. I had given him my heart long ago, and I needed to surrender this endless questioning, too. But sometimes, I thought as I turned in to our driveway, faith is so very hard.

Suddenly I slowed, stopped, and stared at the lawn. Small gray mounds of melting snow. Muddy grass. And there, bravely waving in the wind, one pink crocus.

Hold on, keep going, light is coming soon. There was no way, I knew, that a flower could bloom from a bulb more than eighteen years old, one that had not blossomed in over a decade. But there the crocus was, like a hug from heaven, and tears filled my eyes as I realized its significance. God had heard. And he loved me, so much that he had sent the reassurance I needed in a tenderly personal way, so there would be no doubt.

Moreover, I knew in a shining instant that this was but a taste. Eyes had not seen, minds could not comprehend, the wonders God had planned for his children, and was pouring out on his children— not only in eternity, but *here*, every day. We needed only to listen and look, and cling to him with all our strength, to be part of it all.

The pink crocus bloomed for only one day. April 4. My father's birthday.

But it built my faith for a lifetime.

INTRODUCTION

I will pour out
my spirit upon all mankind.
Your sons and daughters shall prophesy,
your old men shall dream dreams,
your [children] shall see visions;
Even upon the servants and the handmaids,
in those days, I will pour out my spirit.
And I will work wonders in the heavens and on the earth, ...
Then everyone shall be rescued
who calls on the name of the Lord.

—JOEL 3:1–3, 5

Signs and wonders—as intimate as a flower at one moment, at other moments majestic and powerful, but always providing outward evidence of the unseen reality: God is near. Although faith should never depend on such things, we are mystical as well as physical beings, and we need a touch of the sacred now and then to remind us of our eternal home.

However, many believe that signs and wonders are occurring more frequently today. They note a subtle undercurrent of heavenly awareness and activity, perhaps the seeds of a spiritual renaissance, being experienced not just by seers but by the rank and file. In a June 1992 report, the Princeton Religion Research Center found that "seven in ten Americans say their faith has changed significantly, with equal proportions saying it came about as a result of a lot of thought and discussion [or] as a result of a strong emotional experience."

Of course, such things do go in cycles. If we trace the history of Christianity, for example, we see that the charismatic gifts, such as prophecy, visions, and speaking in tongues, faded after the first centuries, giving rise to a more structured church community. Gradually humankind shifted from a constant awareness of the divine to a more scientific emphasis, culminating in the eighteenth century's Age of Reason. Eventually "the supernatural became folklore, relegated to the dustbin of superstition, and ridiculed," explains Michael Brown, author of *The Trumpet of Gabriel*. "Who needed God's light? When man wanted light, he now walked to a switch and turned on the electricity."

But as we reached more recent times, there were indications that ignoring the "God-shaped hole within us" (which, as philosopher Blaise Pascal noted, cannot be filled with anything but God) was not working. Society, with its increase in crime and poverty, its lowering of moral standards, families at risk, promiscuity, racial divisions, and pervasive despair, seemed out of control, at some kind of critical threshold.

It was then, many believe, that a reappraisal began. What was missing? And was a concerned heavenly Father actually sending specific signals, wake-up calls to convince the oblivious and skeptical that our priorities had gotten skewed, that it was necessary to "seek *first* the Kingdom of God"? After a near-death experience (NDE), author Roberts Liardon described this view very specifically: "I was told that [in a period coming soon] God would pour out his spirit on *everyone*; we all would come into contact with the power of the Lord in some way. People would then be faced with a choice, as to what and whether to believe. A surge of manifestation of God's power would come on the youth, both male and female. They would have visions, supernatural dreams, and prophecy."[1]

It seems to be happening. "We live in an exceptional time," said Dr. Peter Wagner, professor of church growth at Fuller Theological Seminary in Pasadena, California, in an April 10, 1995, interview with *Time* magazine. "In the Middle Ages in Europe, perhaps, there may have been something comparable. But certainly in the history of the United States we have never seen such a frequency of signs and wonders." That *Time* and other major media outlets would be covering this topic at all is indicative of the truth of Wagner's statement.

Of course, many people are hesitant about signs and wonders, miracles and other subjective experiences, fearing that they might be associated with serious spiritual error, fraud, or even occult practices. Such concern is necessary, and we should always pray to discern such manifestations correctly. But although there undoubtedly are false miracles—and false prophets—these should not negate the things of heaven. Supernatural signs and wonders do seem to be increasing. So what exactly are we seeing today?

Life Hereafter

Consider the growing awareness and acknowledgment of NDEs, first chronicled by Drs. Raymond Moody and Elisabeth Kübler-Ross in the 1970s. Although considered by some scientists as mere chemical changes in the brain, NDEs nonetheless gained validity as millions reported the death process as visiting a glorious place of light. Ultimately, instead of a final judgment, these witnesses say, God permitted them to return to earth because of work left undone or family responsibilities. "Then I knew. I had to go back. Someone who loved me still needed me," wrote the late Catherine Marshall, depicting her mother's near-death experience in the award-winning book *Christy*. "The light was not for me. Not yet. But sometime. Oh, *sometime*!"

Characteristically, those who have experienced NDEs undergo a spiritual renewal. Most also say they have lost their fear of death, because of a wonderful reassurance that this life is not all there is. And their accounts are particularly consoling for survivors who have lost loved ones, especially under difficult circumstances. Physician Ron Kennedy, attacked in his home after returning from a business trip, described an actual *stopping* of the material world (and his own pain and fear), replaced by a feeling of being surrounded by "a sea of enormous love. It has occurred to me that if this light could appear to me, then those people you love who have died, and maybe in the most extreme circumstances, did not die alone as you would fear that they did: they died with great love around, and peace as well."[2]

An interesting offshoot of the NDE is a circumstance called nearing death awareness (NDA), when dying people seem to interact with heaven in a visionary way. Such episodes were once dismissed as hallucinations, but are now increasingly chronicled by both laypeople and medical personnel.

NDA occurs most typically when a dying person, often wearing a look of wonder and joy, begins to reach, smile, wave, or even talk with someone invisible to others. An elderly man described people sitting with him in quiet comfort, but explained that he was not permitted to tell his daughter who they were. "Do you recognize them?" she asked.

"Of course I do," the father responded, "and the music is beautiful!"

"These [happenings] give us glimpses of whatever dimension exists beyond the life we know," says Maggie Callanan, author of *Final Gifts*, a book about NDA, "and show us how we might take comfort from these reunions and messages."

Angels around Us

In 1991, in my introduction to *Where Angels Walk*, I wrote, "Angels don't get much attention today." Was I wrong! Although I didn't yet know it, a force was gathering and would soon explode into a huge international trend. From it have come television documentaries, stores specializing in angel items, countless books on the subject, and most encouraging, a growing army of witnesses testifying to personal angel encounters and resulting spiritual growth—in a secular, disbelieving world—just as biblical figures did. Hero pilot Scott O'Grady, rescued from enemy territory in Bosnia in April 1995, willingly told the media about a voice and a "protective presence" that kept him reassured during those difficult days. "An Angel Brings Rescuer to Victims" declared a no-longer unusual front-page headline in the Canton, Ohio, *Repository* on December 26, 1994. The most recent polls on this topic, done by Fox News and Gallup, each revealed that over 75 percent of Americans now believe in angels.

Why the interest? Perhaps more relevant: Why now? "The world is filled with spiritual warfare," said Bishop Job, of the Midwest Russian Orthodox Church of America, in a recent video on angels.[3] "We see it in every aspect of our society, of current affairs. . . . Life has become a complete tension between good and evil." People are putting their trust in the natural world where they can easily be led astray, he believes, rather than in God and what God has revealed. Perhaps God is sending angels to remind us of these errors, and to draw our attention back to spiritual concerns.

Clouds of Witnesses

In addition to angels, some people believe they have experienced unexpected contact with loved ones now in heaven. Events such as these were once considered grief-induced fantasies, and kept secret—it is one thing to believe, however tentatively, that God might send an angel to bring comfort or help someone in need. But to send those now living in eternity? Hardly.

However, with near-death and angel experiences gaining credibility, society seems to be awakening to other mystical possibilities. "Once we accept that a light can come to us when we die, and we can interact with that light, we must . . . [recognize] that that same light can interact with us at other times during our lives," says Melvin Morse, MD, pediatrician and author of *Final Visions*. Because our culture rarely allows for the idea of heaven and earth intersecting, Morse claims that this is "in many ways . . . a harder concept to accept than life after death."

And yet St. Paul referred to that great "cloud of witnesses" who, now in heaven, stand ready to help and reassure us as we complete our earthly mission. Why would God not occasionally permit us to be touched by them?

Dreams and Visions

Our Father has always reached his people in this way; at least seventy passages or events in the Bible refer to dreams and visions, promised by God as early as the days of Moses. "Should there be a prophet among you, in visions will I reveal myself to him, in dreams will I speak to him" (Numbers 12:6). Those skilled in interpreting dreams and visions were revered, and church fathers paid serious attention to them. However, as faith became more ritualized, many leaders relegated dreams and visions to the world of superstition.

But "so far we haven't found anything in nature that doesn't have its function," wrote John Sanford in *Dreams: God's Forgotten Language*. "So why should we say that of all created things, the dream alone makes no sense?" Since dreams are not necessarily limited by time and space or barriers that humankind deliberately erects, Sanford points out, it's a natural way for God to reach us.

Visions are another way. Who can overlook the dramatic increase in reported apparitions of Mary, the Mother of Jesus (almost two hundred reputed new sightings just in the past few years), and related phenomena, such as weeping or moving statues, spinning suns, and other occurrences? And "Catholics aren't the only seers," noted Robert Ellwood, professor of comparative religion at the University of Southern California, in the *Los Angeles Times* (July 13, 1994). "Protestants have visions of angels or Jesus, Hindus have visions of Krishna." Since 1990, reports of similar happenings have come from Iraq, Syria, Israel, Korea, India, and Lebanon; accounts of apparitions involving former Muslims have surfaced in Kenya, while in Nepal, large numbers of Hindus reported seeing the image of a crucified man in the sky. A Greek Orthodox church in Chicago, typical of many such sites, contains a painting that shed tears for seven months in 1986, and attracted over four million visitors, including scientists and representatives from the Smithsonian Institute. Witnesses to the occurrence reported many physical and emotional healings.

Although a number of these happenings are ultimately found to be fraudulent or explainable by natural means—and church leaders maintain a healthy skepticism about most others—it's obvious that the sheer number of such reports is increasing. Why? Messages (when provided) are remarkably similar: God is urging repentance, pouring out his mercy on the entire world, and calling his children to his side. It's not the phenomenon itself that is important, say experts, but what it means and where it leads.

Changes in Nature

Six of the ten costliest disasters in U.S. history have occurred since 1989 (four since 1992), including the Los Angeles earthquake, the 1993 Mississippi River floods, which inundated an area the size of Switzerland, and three years ago, Hurricane Katrina, which left thousands of people homeless. An estimated 1,167 tornadoes were reported in the U.S. in 1993; 1995 was the most active East Coast hurricane season in more than forty years. In early 1996, several areas of the country endured record snowfalls and floods. Droughts seem to be increasing in both number and intensity. Has this all some spiritual significance? Are such phenomena fulfilling prophecies from earlier times?

We know that a loving Father would not deliberately *send* such devastation, any more than human parents would intentionally inflict pain on their offspring. But wise adults do permit children to experience the consequences of their behavior, as learning tools. Might

God now be simply lifting the protective hand that he has long held over us, as a demonstration of what *could* happen if we continue to ignore him? "When mankind rejects God, it is also rejecting the force that binds the universe and keeps everything from chaos," believes author Michael Brown. "But as at Sodom and Gomorrah, God's warnings are almost always conditional. They describe what will happen *if* present circumstances persist."

It is easy to see the negative side of nature out of control. But consider an interesting aspect: in many recent disasters there has been destruction to *property*, but a less-than-expected death and injury toll. One homeowner, surveying the smoldering remains of the Oakland, California, fires, summed it up: "I suddenly realized that everything that *man* had made was gone. Yet everything that God had made—our faith, our spirit, the love and support all around us, even the little flowers bravely pushing through the ashes—all this was still here." For this man, the fire had become a blessing that forced him to reevaluate his life and his priorities.

On other occasions, people have treated approaching storms or floods as faith builders, by praying fervently that God put a ring of protection around their home or farm. Stories abound of hurricanes suddenly changing course or crops remaining safe despite freezing temperatures. Coincidences? Perhaps. Or perhaps these, too, are just part of the wonders God is showing us today.

The Power of Prayer

Years ago we might have assumed that miracles were possible but granted only at distant shrines or through an anointed few, surely not for ordinary folks like us. Today we are learning that such a philosophy is too limited. "I was ready to respond to those who asked me not," God reminds us in the book of Isaiah (65:1). "I said: 'Here I am, here I am,' to a nation that did not call upon my name." Our Father wants us to ask, even boldly, for what we need, because asking is a sign that we understand our relationship with him.

Over one hundred scientific experiments have already been done on this theme, showing that prayer does bring about significant changes, especially when used in physical and emotional healings. "If the technique being studied had been a new drug or a surgical procedure instead of prayer, it would have been heralded as some sort of breakthrough," notes Dr. Larry Dossey, author of *Healing Words*.

"My sense is that the healing phenomenon is the next phase of Jewish spirituality," adds Rabbi Michael Swarttz, executive director of Camp Ramah, a Jewish healing center in Palmer, Massachusetts. "It involves people who are seeking and looking for ways to connect to God."

That's why today people routinely pray over those who are ill, asking God for multiplication miracles, including taking command over nature. Why membership in praise communities, prayer groups, and other more active and dynamic forms of worship is growing. Why some children—in many cultures, considered to have a special link with the sacred—seem to have spiritual wisdom beyond their years, just as the Book of Joel predicted. Why miracles seem to be happening more frequently than ever before.

And that's why people of many ages and faiths have been willing to share their own glimpses of heaven on the following pages.* Although some of these events happened years ago, the majority are recent occurrences, offering reassuring evidence that God has not abandoned his people. Instead, he continues to call us—with little signs or awesome wonders—every day of our lives.

*Note: An asterisk (*) after a name indicates the name has been changed.

FOR LOVE OF LOGAN

Jesus said to them, . . . "Go and tell John what you hear and see: the blind regain their sight, the lame walk, lepers are cleansed, the deaf hear, the dead are raised."

—MATTHEW 11:4–5

Tami Carroll grew up in a small Indiana town, married in 1986 shortly after her high school graduation, and had her first baby, Jaclyn, a few years later. "It was a routine pregnancy and delivery, no trouble at all," Tami recalls. She and husband Todd settled into a peaceful life on their farm, enjoying parenthood and planning a larger family. There was no warning of what was to come.

Tami became pregnant again in 1993. Everything seemed normal until her sixth month, when an ultrasound revealed problems. Tami's obstetrician, Dr. Diana Okon, gently broke the news. "The baby had chromosomal abnormalities, stemming from a condition that is always fatal," Dr. Okon says. The child, a girl, would die either during the next few months, or shortly after birth.

Tami and Todd were heartbroken. They named their unborn daughter Megan, and hoped she knew how much they loved her. Eventually Tami gave birth, but there was little to celebrate, for baby Megan was stillborn. "My mother had died when I was twenty," Tami said, "and at the time I thought there could be no greater pain than losing a parent. But now I had to admit that the pain of losing a child was even worse." Also difficult was the seed of doubt that had been planted. Could this happen again—did the Carrolls have some kind of genetic defect? Worse, what if Megan was the last child they would ever conceive?

Tests on Tami and Todd showed nothing amiss, however, and eventually Tami became pregnant again. But now she was nervous, afraid to get her hopes up. In addition, although Tami had grown up as a Southern Baptist, she hadn't been to church in years. "For many reasons, I had sort of given up on God," she admits. "At times, I felt that even if he was listening to me, he probably didn't care." But gradually, as this pregnancy progressed, Tami found herself talking to her heavenly Father. "God, please give me a healthy baby," she asked each day, Megan's death still fresh in her mind. Even if she and God had not been close for a while, he surely wouldn't ask her to go through another loss like that, would he?

Time passed, and despite her worry, Tami had no problems. Dr. Okon monitored her carefully, doing a chromosomal test as well as extra ultrasounds. The baby—a boy whom the Carrolls had already named Logan—looked vital and completely normal.

Tami was due on April 9, 1995. But when she went to the office for her scheduled checkup on April 5, Dr. Okon decided to hospitalize her early the next morning. "I think she knew I was worried and that it might be better for me to be induced in a controlled setting," Tami explains.

The following morning, Todd and Tami drove to Clark Memorial Hospital in nearby Jeffersonville. Tami was admitted, labor began, and everything seemed fine. Baby Logan was closely monitored, and his heart was healthy and strong. Todd and Ruthie, Tami's sister, were with her, and as things progressed, the grandparents assembled in the waiting room. It would be a joyous event—not like the last time, they all assured each other. New life was budding. Logan was almost here!

By late afternoon, Dr. Okon had delivered two other babies and was as ready as Tami to meet little Logan. Her contractions strong and healthy, Tami was taken to the delivery room. She was almost to the end now, and as the nurses cheered her on, she pushed and pushed. "One more!" a nurse shouted. "He's almost here!" Tami pushed again. But Logan's heart rate had suddenly slowed. And at 4:42, as Dr. Okon took him from the womb, there was no heartbeat at all. "There was a loose umbilical cord around the infant's neck that slid off easily. [His] mouth and nose were bulb-suctioned on the perineum and the fluid was clear," Dr. Okon wrote in a later report. But the baby's Apgar score—the test that determines newborn health—was zero. He wasn't breathing.

"Call code," Dr. Okon quickly told a nurse as she carried the lifeless infant to the warmer on the other side of the room and gave him oxygen. "Come on, Logan!" she murmured. "Wake up!" Another nurse started chest compressions.

There was no cry, no heartbeat, no pulse. The baby's eyes remained closed, his limbs limp, his color an unhealthy gray.

"Logan?" Tami asked. "Todd, why isn't he crying?"

Todd stood in shock, watching nurses running here and there. No one was saying anything, and the silence was horrible. *Logan, Logan, please cry.* Ruthie realized something terrible was happening and hurriedly left the room.

Within seconds, it seemed, an emergency room physician raced in, followed by Tami's pediatrician, who had been summoned from her nearby office. One of the nurses phoned Kosair Children's Hospital in nearby Louisville, Kentucky, which has a neonatal unit and specialists on call. A respiratory therapist passed Tami, then an X-ray technician. "What is going on?" Tami screamed, beginning to sob. Tears streamed down Todd's cheeks.

A nurse tried to comfort them. "We don't know anything yet," she whispered.

It couldn't be happening, not again. She couldn't lose another child. *Logan, please breathe.*

Dr. Okon came to Tami's side, to finish the delivery process. The specialists, she explained softly, had intubated the baby and were forcing air into his lungs. Someone had injected medication, someone else was taking X-rays, everything possible was being done. To Tami, it was all a horrible nightmare. She had thought everything was under control, and now she realized that nothing was. Only God could help Logan now. "Dear God," she whispered through her tears, "please don't do this. I don't think I can handle it. Please save Logan, please. I'll take him in any condition."

Medical personnel continued to work over the baby. "But Logan never showed any signs of life, nor did he respond to any of the advanced cardiac life-support efforts by the code team," says Dr. Okon. At 5:15, thirty-five minutes after delivery, the neonatal specialists from Kosair and Clarke Hospital personnel agreed to discontinue all resuscitation efforts. Logan was pronounced dead.

Unobtrusively, a nurse baptized Logan. Another weighed him— eight pounds, three ounces—cleaned him, wrapped him in warm blankets, put a little stocking cap on his dark head, and laid him in Tami's arms for a last good-bye. She held him close, searching his perfect little face. "Logan, don't go—I need you," she whispered. But her son's eyes were closed, his body completely limp. *Dear God, please.* She had to let go, to accept the inevitable, but somehow, she couldn't stop praying.

Dr. Okon and the pediatrician stood by Tami's bed; the others had left the delivery room. "We don't know what happened, Tami," Dr. Okon said. "We won't have any answers unless we do an autopsy."

Tami blinked back tears. Perhaps an autopsy would save another family the suffering she was enduring. "All right," she agreed. "But I want to hold him for a while."

"Of course." Someone brought a consent form, and still holding Logan, Tami reached over and signed it. Dr. Okon left the room to break the news to the Carroll relatives in the waiting room. Soon they streamed in, murmuring words of encouragement, mingling their tears with Tami's and Todd's.

Todd cuddled Logan, then passed him to Ruthie. The nurse took some photographs. Occasionally the baby's body moved slightly, and the first time it happened, the nurse went out to the front desk and alerted Dr. Okon, who was talking to another physician on the phone. Dr. Okon explained that such a phenomenon was called "agonal breathing," and was just a spasm or a reaction to the medication the baby had received. How unfortunate, she thought, that the Carrolls had seen it—it was almost like Logan dying twice.

At 5:55 p.m., mourning was coming to an end, at least for the moment. It was time, everyone knew, to turn Logan's body over to the hospital. Tami's stepmother was holding him, and she bent over him to say a last good-bye. Once again, his little body went into a spasm. Tami's stepmother looked, and looked again. "Tami, he—he's gasping!" she cried. "Look, his leg moved!"

"It's just a spasm, like the nurse said," Tami answered.

"I don't think so—I think he's breathing," Grandma exclaimed. "Ruthie, get a nurse!"

Ruthie did. In an attempt to calm the family, the same nurse came quickly and put her fingertips on the baby's chest. Then she reached for a stethoscope and listened. "Wait right here!" she shouted, as she ran out of the room.

Dr. Okon was still filling out forms when the excited nurse approached her. "She said, 'The Carroll baby has a heartbeat,' and I responded, 'The next one to have a heart attack is going to be me if this doesn't stop,'" Dr. Okon reports. But when she reached the now silent room and approached Tami's stepmother, she could see that the baby was turning pink. "He's alive?" she asked the older woman.

Tami's stepmother could only nod, her arms trembling. Astonished, Dr. Okon took the baby from her. His little chest was rising and falling rapidly. "He is alive!" she cried. "Let's take him to the nursery!" Nurse and physician ran with the infant out of the room.

Tami began to weep. She had been grieving for over an hour for her child, and now, it seemed, the cycle had started over. "Don't do this again—I can't lose him twice!" she wept, as Todd, still thunderstruck, tried to comfort her.

"We don't know what's going on, Tami," he explained.

Tami did. It was just a cruel joke. For some reason Logan's little body was still reacting to treatment, and everyone thought . . . But such things were impossible! Her son had been dead for an hour and eighteen minutes—no one could come back to life after all that time.

And yet, she had asked God for a miracle, hadn't she?

Medical personnel began reappearing in the delivery room with bulletins for Tami and Todd. The neonatologists from Kosair Children's Hospital had returned, dumbfounded. They were currently examining Logan in the nursery. His disbelieving pediatrician was also there, along with doctors from all over the hospital, responding to the quickly spreading news. Despite the impossibility of it, Logan was breathing on his own and appeared healthy. He had been placed in an oxygen tent, and tests were proceeding.

Of course, there were undertones that were not mentioned, at least not at this joyful, exultant moment. A baby clinically dead for over an hour would no doubt have severe brain damage, as well as nonfunctioning optic nerves, tissue damage, seizures—the list could be endless. But Tami was joyful. She had told God she would love Logan no matter what, and she intended to keep her promise. For now, everyone was in a state of awe. It was, as Dr. Okon described it later, like seeing the shadow of God passing by.

Baby Logan was transferred to Kosair Children's Hospital and remained there for five weeks. He slept for the first two, due to medication reducing the possibility of seizures, and then gradually began to awaken. Although brain-damaged babies often don't suck, he nursed immediately. Tests showed that his eyes and hearing were completely normal.

The story touched many. Medical personnel at Clarke Hospital dubbed him "Lazarus." Strangers approached Tami on the street with tears in their eyes. Even an elderly lady wrote to tell the Carrolls that the same thing had happened to her at birth, and no one had ever believed her mother—until now.

What happened to this very special baby? No one really knows. One theory is that Logan might have experienced the same kind of situation as a drowning victim—when systems shut down for a time, then spontaneously revive. However, Logan had never actually *been* alive after birth, and Dr. Okon, who has seen nothing like it in her years of practice, is grateful that she was not the only specialist on the scene. "If I had been alone," she told Tami, "I might have concluded that I had made a mistake, missed a tiny sign of life. But there were other physicians there, including neonatologists, and we all agreed." Logan was dead, and then he was resurrected.

Today Logan, diagnosed with cerebral palsy several years ago, has a rich and satisfying life. Despite being confined to a wheelchair, he is bright and fun loving, attends a regular school, and is an inspiration to everyone who meets him. Onlookers might wonder why Logan was not completely healed. But those who know Tami and the unconditional love that she has always given her son understand that *this* is the best part of the miracle.

Why did it happen? "Maybe God wanted to show us that miracles do happen, to say, 'I'm still here and I still raise people from the dead,'" Tami says. "And maybe it's not my job to ask why, but just to keep telling others, and keep saying thank you."

She is willing to carry out that heavenly assignment. What else can one do with such a wonder?

MIRACLE IN MOBILE

The gloriously odd may be more normal than we think.

—TIMOTHY JONES, *CELEBRATION OF ANGELS*

For some of us, signs and wonders are rare events (at least it seems that way). Others, like Betty Billings, have had a lifetime of spiritual adventures. Hers began when she was six, and had a near-death experience while her tonsils were being removed. The voice of a gentle, loving man spoke to her in the midst of an exquisite meadowlike setting—a scene she has never seen duplicated, despite her extensive travels. She believes she was in heaven with Jesus, and he gave her a choice to return to earth.

After her marriage, Betty worked a construction job. On one occasion, at a building site, a scaffold board weighing over two hundred pounds fell from above, right toward her head. "Look out!" the other workers yelled at Betty, and she jumped away. But not before all of them saw the board stop in midair—for just a few seconds—before crashing to the spot where she had been.

Perhaps Betty's most wondrous adventure happened in 1956. She lived in Cincinnati and had been moping ever since her best friends Pat and Sam Brewer* had moved to Mobile, Alabama. When her husband, Kenneth, came home one night, Betty had a plan. "We need a vacation," she announced. "Let's drive down and visit the Brewers for the Fourth of July weekend."

Kenneth looked dubiously at their two-year-old son. "Wouldn't it be a long ride for Timothy?"

"Probably," Betty said, nodding, "but I miss Pat and Sam so much." Although the couples kept in touch, phone calls couldn't substitute for being together.

There were no interstate highways then, and the following day when Kenneth brought home a map, he realized that the journey to Mobile would take almost twenty hours. Worse, they'd arrive toward evening, and the Brewers lived in an obscure area. Betty had called the Brewers that day; they were delighted at the upcoming visit, and suggested Kenneth phone when he reached Mobile so they could provide specific directions to their home. But Kenneth was still concerned about getting lost.

Betty, however, had no such qualms, and was delightedly immersed in packing. "God will be watching over us," she told her hesitant husband. "You know I try to keep him as close as my tongue and my car keys! It will all work out."

The drive was long and tedious, and they stopped frequently so Timothy could run around. But only when they drove into Mobile on Highway 45 and found themselves in a darkening, run-down section of town did Betty begin to worry. The map did seem very confusing. Apparently a river was ahead of them, and then what? "God, we need help," Betty whispered.

Coming up on their right was a Pure Oil station. It looked closed, since there were no customers buying gas at the pumps, no activity of any kind inside the brick building. But perhaps there would be a pay phone available. Kenneth turned in, and as he did, a slim blue-uniformed attendant appeared, striding briskly toward their car. "We're a little lost," Kenneth told him.

"How can I help?" The attendant looked through the window, smiling at Timothy.

Kenneth gave him Sam's address, and the attendant nodded. "You go down here." He pointed confidently, without consulting the map. "And then—" His directions were brief, businesslike, and easy to understand.

What a nice man, Betty thought. *There's no need to call the Brewers now.* Wearily she leaned back and closed her eyes. Odd, though, that a mechanic's clothes would be this crisp and clean so late in the day. And the man had appeared so quickly, almost as if he was *expecting* them.

But his directions were perfect. Soon Kenneth and Betty pulled up in front of a small house, and Pat and Sam ran down the front walk, arms wide in welcome. "Why didn't you phone us?" Pat asked when the hugging stopped. "Our house is so hard to find."

"We didn't need to—the Pure Oil attendant in town knew exactly where you lived," Kenneth explained.

"Who?"

Betty described the station, the specific corner, the helpful man who seemed to know what they needed before they'd even asked. Only then did she notice the odd looks on Pat's and Sam's faces.

"Betty," Pat said gently. "You couldn't have gotten directions there."

"But we did," Betty insisted.

"No." Pat shook her head. "There *used* to be a Pure Oil station at that intersection. But it was torn down several years ago to widen the highway. There's just a little part of one brick wall left."

Betty bit her tongue. She didn't want to argue, not after such an exhausting journey. She would simply show her friends tomorrow.

The next day, however, there was nothing to show. Although Betty and Kenneth remembered their route and retraced it to the same corner, they found no service station, no gas pumps, no blue-uniformed attendant. Just weeds—and part of an old brick wall.

The Billingses moved to Mobile the following year. And whenever Betty passed "her" corner, she felt an unmistakable glow. Had it been a vision, that glimpse into a time long ago? She couldn't explain it. She knew only that she had asked God to protect her family. And he had shown her that wherever his children travel, they are never alone.

INVISIBLE GUARDIANS

It was as if an incandescent delight had entered through his eyes and filtered through to illuminate every molecule of his being.

—ETHEL POCHOCKI, *THE WIND HARP AND OTHER ANGEL TALES*

Twenty-five-year-old Dave Carr of Bangor, Maine, was feeling one of those inner urges that defy logic and reason. He had a strong impulse to open a gathering place for the homeless, or people down on their luck. "I thought of providing them with a soft drink or coffee and something to eat, along with a hug and some words of encouragement," Dave says. "Most important, I wanted them to learn about the Bible, and hopefully to accept Jesus into their hearts."

This "heavenly nudge" grew stronger over the next several years. But Dave argued with it. How could *he* open such a place? True, he had always lived a life of service and had helped on similar projects through his church. But he was a truck driver, not a minister or psychologist, and he had a young family to support, with nothing left over for rent on a drop-in center. The whole idea was impossible.

But Dave continued to think about it. Street people led hard lives, he knew; not only were they hungry and often cold in Maine's hard climate, they were vulnerable to threats from those stronger than they. Recently a man had been murdered in the middle of the night, and thrown over the bridge into the Penobscot River. The police had not found his attackers. And without some kind of safe oasis, Dave thought, such a thing was sure to happen again.

Finally Dave drove to downtown Bangor about 10:00 p.m. one September evening. It wouldn't hurt to at least *look* at possible sites. "I need nighttime hours to think quietly, and I thought it would be easier to check out storefronts without being distracted by traffic," he says. He parked and walked through the neighborhoods, looking at abandoned buildings. Some possibilities, but nothing definite.

At 1:00 a.m. Dave was ready to call it quits. But he hadn't investigated Brewer yet, the city that lies across the Penobscot River from Bangor. He would look at a few sites there, then head home.

The street was deserted as Dave started walking up the bridge. Then a car approached from Brewer. As its headlights caught him, the car slowed. Uneasily Dave realized that there were three men inside. Despite the cool night air, their windows were rolled down. "Let's throw him over!" Dave heard one of them say. The car stopped, its doors opened, and all three jumped out and came toward him.

Horrified, Dave suddenly recalled the murder of the street person. It had been on this bridge! Had these men done it? He would be no match for them, he knew—his only option was to pray that he survived the icy water. But as he looked down, he realized that the tide had gone out, and only rocks and dirt were directly below him. "God, help me," Dave murmured.

Immediately he felt a presence near him, something unseen but definitely *there*. A warm, safe feeling flooded him. His fear vanished, and he knew, without knowing quite how he knew, that he was not alone.

Now the men were almost upon Dave. All three were large, muscular—and leering. "Get him!" one shouted.

Suddenly they stopped. "They all stared at me, then looked to the right and left of me," Dave says. "They seemed terrified. One said, 'Oh, my God!' They turned and began shoving one another to get back to the car. And when they sped away—it sounded like they tore the transmission right out—I could still hear them cursing and yelling, 'Run, run!'"

Dave stood for a moment on the deserted bridge, basking in the warmth that still surrounded him. What was it? What had the men seen? Whatever it was, it had shielded him from certain death. "Thank you, God," he whispered.

He felt exalted, so buoyant that he decided to go on to Brewer and finish his search. As he crossed the rest of the bridge, Danny, a friend of his, drove by, honked at him, and kept going, unmindful of Dave's narrow escape. Dave waved, still surrounded by peace.

A while later, Dave came across some derelicts standing on a Brewer street corner. But as he approached, they all fell back.

One put his hands over his eyes. "You're shining!" he whispered. "It hurts to look!"

"I can feel the Holy Spirit all around you!" said another, as he inched away.

Dave was awed. It was *heaven's* glow surrounding him. It had to be! But he wasn't absolutely positive until the next day when he ran into Danny again.

"Sorry I didn't stop for you last night on the bridge," Danny said, "but I had passengers and I never could have fit all of you in my car, too."

"All of us?" Dave asked, puzzled.

"Those three huge guys walking with you," Danny explained. "They were the biggest people I have ever seen. One must have been at least seven feet tall!"

Dave never resisted a heavenly nudge again. He eventually opened and funded a Bangor coffeehouse, which is still running today under a friend's management. At least one hundred people are fed every night, with coffee, hugs—and the word of the Lord.

SURPRISE WITNESS

How great is the wonder of heavenly and earthly things!

—CICERO, *DE NATURA DEORUM*

Peggy Williams was very worried about her daughter, Sherri. After seventeen years of marriage, Sherri had recently gotten a divorce, and the past months had been traumatic for her and her two children. "As a fifth-grade teacher, she had to bear up under a lot of pressure at school," Peggy says. "But she was falling apart emotionally at home due to ongoing harassment from her ex-husband, as well as disrespect from her children, who were upset over the divorce. It all put a heavy strain on her." The women talked often, but Peggy felt helpless to solve Sherri's problems. All she could do was pray with her daughter, hoping the stress would ease.

But a difficult hurdle lay ahead of Sherri: a final court date to determine custody, alimony, and other arrangements. Sherri's husband had warned her he would do "whatever it takes" to get custody of the children. Many in his family, which was well known and influential in the community, were attending this hearing to support him, as they had done in the past. Since Sherri hadn't shared her tales of marital difficulties with friends, she now had no one who could testify on her behalf, other than Tammy, her husband's niece and a good friend. But Tammy's loyalties would certainly be divided, and Sherri wouldn't ask Tammy to choose sides. No, except for her mother, Sherri was alone and she knew it. Her ex-husband was a good father, but despite the children's anger over the divorce, they wanted to stay with her. Yet how could she win them when the odds seemed so stacked against her?

Peggy, of course, would go to court with Sherri. But when the hearing was finally scheduled, there was a conflict. Peggy, a real estate broker, had paid tuition for a course she needed. The date of the hearing—October 5—fell during the week of the course, which was being taught in Norfolk, Virginia, four driving hours away. Peggy was upset, since another course wouldn't be available for months. But she decided to cancel and stay with Sherri.

Sherri objected. "Mom, you have to go ahead with this course," she told Peggy. "We'll talk every night of the week you're gone. Things will work out." Peggy wasn't so sure, but eventually she gave in.

On Monday evening, October 3, Peggy called her daughter. Sherri was calm about the upcoming court date, and Peggy hung up, reassured. But on Tuesday the atmosphere had changed. Sherri was terribly upset about a minor request her lawyer had made, and

Peggy's concern grew. Her daughter had always been so well orga-
nized and capable—this was not at all the Sherri everyone knew.
What if she broke down on the stand, or seemed hysterical? What
chance would she have to win custody? Oh, if only someone could
be there with her! "Sherri, I'll pray all day tomorrow for you," Peggy
told her. It was all she could think of to say.

Peggy was awake most of the night, tossing and turning, wor-
rying about Sherri and the children. "Lord, let her be brave," Peggy
whispered. "Put a partition between Sherri and all those against her
in the courtroom, so she won't see them and be frightened. Help
her, Lord!"

Wednesday morning Peggy went to class, but she barely concentrated on the lessons. Tears sprang to her eyes several times
as she pictured her daughter, lonely and vulnerable, being cross-
examined and denounced. What would Sherri do? What would
happen to the kids?

When break time came at 9:15, Peggy stumbled through the con-
vention hall lobby to an outside terrace, and looked up at the sky.
Sunlight was all around her, yet she felt mired in darkness. She had
to relinquish Sherri to God's care, she knew. Only he could help her
now. "God, I love my child, and I can't be with her," Peggy prayed,
lifting her tearful face to heaven. "So please, will you take over?"

The rest of the day seemed endless, but finally Peggy returned
to her hotel and called Sherri. "Mom! You'll never believe it!"

Sherri's jubilant voice was a shock. "The judge gave me custody! And my lawyer said I received one of the best support settlements he's ever seen!"

"Sherri, that's amazing. What happened?"

"Well, the first odd thing was that when I was testifying, my chair was facing away from everyone who was against me. I couldn't see them at all, so I felt a lot calmer. I could remember words and events with no trouble at all."

Peggy remembered her prayer. *Lord, put a partition between Sherri and those against her.* "That's wonderful, honey. But still, how—"

"It was Tammy, Mom. She came to court at the very last minute, asked the judge if she could be heard, and testified for me. She was wonderful, and I'm sure she was the critical factor in the judge's decision."

Tammy? How unexpected.

"She said that although she loved both her uncle and me, she was most concerned about our children," Sherri went on. "She broke down and cried when she described how they were being pulled apart by this whole thing."

"But why?" Peggy asked. "What made Tammy decide to come, especially at the very last minute?"

"Why?" Sherri sounded puzzled. "Why, Mom, *you* did."

"I?"

"Yes. Tammy said you phoned and told her to get up, and don't take time to dress up—just put on anything—and get down to the courthouse because your grandchildren needed her. Tammy tried to argue with you, but you were so firm about it that she gave up and came. She even took her three-year-old with her. It was *you*, Mom."

Peggy's knees were weak. "What time did Tammy receive this call?" she asked.

"It was 9:15 exactly."

Nine-fifteen. The moment when Peggy had turned her tear-streaked face to heaven, and asked God to take over. She had been nowhere near a phone then, of course, nor did she know Tammy's unlisted number. Nor would it have occurred to her to involve Tammy. But what were such limits to God?

"Things are better for all of us now," Peggy reports. "We do a lot of praying, and we constantly search the word for answers and direction. But this experience has been something that neither of us will ever forget."

MESSENGER FROM CORK

We are never so lost that our angels cannot find us.

—STEPHANIE POWERS, *ANGELS II: BEYOND THE LIGHT*

As spring break approached at the University of London, American student Kelley O'Connell decided to take advantage of a unique opportunity. What more perfect time to visit Ireland, the country of her ancestors?

Kelley had always been concerned about not having enough money. "When you're raised in a family that's struggling financially, you worry," she says. But college students typically travel on slim budgets, especially in Europe where youth hostels charge just a few dollars a night. So although Kelly flew to Dublin with only about $275, and her bus and train passes, she felt confident.

She took in the sights in Dublin, stayed in a hostel, and rode the train down to Cork the next morning. But that night Kelley opened her knapsack and discovered that she had been robbed—her roll of cash was gone! The familiar panic rolled over her. She had about thirty dollars in her jeans pocket, and some bread and granola in her bag, not enough to live on for another week. Her airline ticket to London was good only on the date issued. What would she do? Kelley placed a collect call to her parents in Omaha, but they were on vacation. "I'll try to find them," her brother promised, "but you probably won't receive any money until Monday or Tuesday."

How would she live in the meantime? This long-awaited dream trip was becoming a nightmare.

Determined to salvage what she could, Kelley continued traveling during the following days. She eventually reached her father, who promised to have money at an American Express office in Limerick on Wednesday. "In the meantime," he advised her, "why don't you go to a church? I'm sure someone there would help."

No. Kelley appreciated his advice, but she wouldn't take it. "I had rejected my Catholic upbringing when I was sixteen," she says. "To me, religion was just a bunch of rules. I was an angry, independent adolescent who wasn't sure what I believed, but I had no spiritual connection. The only time I ever acknowledged God was when I was mad at him. If something went wrong, it was his fault. Otherwise, he didn't exist." She'd feel like a hypocrite if she went to a church now.

But when she found herself on a park bench in Limerick in the cold, rainy darkness, Kelley realized she had reached a dead end. She had eighty cents in her pocket, and six days before her return flight to London. Her money was due to arrive tomorrow afternoon—but what if it didn't? She was alone in an unfamiliar city with nowhere to stay, and to top everything off, today was her twenty-first birthday. What a cruel joke!

Tears filled her eyes. "Across the street was a youth hostel," she says. "I knew it would be closing about nine—they all did—so I took a deep breath and knocked on the door." When the proprietor came, she explained her situation. "I'd be happy to clean for you tomorrow, in exchange for lodging tonight," she suggested.

"We're barely open—there are only two guests here," he answered. "Why don't you ask for help at the church down the street?"

Not again! Kelley shook her head firmly.

"Well, come in," he sighed. "I'll find some work for you to do."

He gave Kelley a room on floor two, the women's floor (men were on floor three). She met the other two guests, "but I sensed that they had nothing to spare, so I didn't tell them anything," she says. Eventually the couple went out for a walk. The owner had gone to his quarters after locking the front door, so Kelley was alone. Slumping miserably in the lounge, she ate the remainder of her bread and granola while tears rolled down her cheeks. *Happy birthday to me.* She had never felt so lonely.

At 10:00 p.m. the lounge door opened unexpectedly, and a man walked in. "Okay if I sit down?" he asked her.

Kelley looked up. He was tall, slim, and young, with coal-black wavy hair and pale Irish skin. "But it was his eyes that caught my attention," Kelley says. "They were the brightest, most beautiful blue I'd ever seen. They seemed old and young at the same time."

The man put out his hand. "I'm Peter McGucky." He smiled.

"Kelley O'Connell, from London University." Kelley blinked back tears.

"I've been living in London, too," Peter explained, "but I'm moving back to my brother's house in Cork and doing some sightseeing on the way. Why are you crying?"

Kelley told him. "Hmmm." Peter's face grew thoughtful. "Don't worry, love. I'll stay with you until we get it all straightened out. Everything will be all right. You'll see."

Kelley was already relaxing. Peter's very presence was calming. The two began to talk of trivial things, of daily life, of plans and hopes. "There was nothing significant in our conversation," Kelley says, "but its very ordinariness seemed to reduce my tension." Tomorrow, Peter reassured her, they would go to the American Express office, and her father's package would be there. Nothing to worry about.

The following day Kelley awakened early and did her assigned chores. The other two boarders left, and eventually Kelley tiptoed up to the third floor to find Peter's room and remind him about their trip to the American Express office. But all the rooms were empty. Puzzled, Kelley went downstairs and found the innkeeper. "Where's Peter?" she asked.

"Who?"

"Peter McGucky. The dark-haired man. The one who checked in late last night."

The owner gave Kelley a skeptical look. "You were the only arrival last night," he told her. "And there's no guest named Peter here." Looking over his shoulder, he moved quickly away from her.

"But—" Kelley looked up. *There* was Peter, standing on the upstairs landing, smiling down at her. "You look like you could use some breakfast," he said as he came down the stairs. "Here, you can share mine."

Kelley kept thinking of her encounter with the innkeeper. Who could overlook someone like Peter? But she ate gladly, and soon she and Peter were strolling across Limerick to the American Express office, a tiny glassed-in storefront with one entrance, in front.

Peter waited outside while Kelley went in to sign for her package. But another difficulty lay ahead. "We've already received today's delivery from America," the lady explained. "There was nothing in it for you."

Oh no! Not another day of being penniless! The familiar hysteria gripped Kelley and then, somehow, seemed to recede. Even inside the little office, she could feel Peter's calmness settling around her. Hadn't he said that everything would work out? She decided to trust. "What should I do?" she asked the clerk.

Phone calls were made, tracers started, a driver alerted. "You're in luck," the clerk finally told Kelley. "They found the misdirected package, and the truck is on its way back. You might as well wait outside; it may take a while." Kelley went out to explain things to Peter. Once again, she felt no distress, just a simple awe at how things seemed to be falling into place.

The two talked casually. It was a beautiful day; odd that she had not noticed until now.

"And then," Kelley says, "although we had been standing right in front of the shop, and no one had gone in or out, nor had any truck pulled up, the clerk came out. 'Your package just came!' she told me."

It was impossible. But there was her father's familiar handwriting, and inside, the cash she needed to complete her vacation. Somehow it had reached this obscure store without them noticing. But how?

She and Peter went to lunch, then strolled to the bus stop. "I'll be going back and forth between Cork and London a few more times," he told her as he wrote his brother's address on a piece of paper. "He doesn't have a phone, but here's where I'll be."

Kelley gave him her London address. There were no words to tell him how grateful she was. His emotional and moral support was just what she had needed.

Peter hugged her. "In spite of it all, you could have gone to the church," he said gently. "It will always accept you, you know."

"Yes. I know." Somehow she had always known it. She turned away and boarded her bus.

The remainder of Kelley's trip went well, and after she returned to London, she sent money and a letter of thanks to Peter at his brother's Cork address.

A week later her letter came back. "No such name," it was stamped. "No existing address."

Kelley stared at the letter. And suddenly it struck her. All the discrepancies she had ignored—Peter entering a locked hostel, the proprietor not seeing him, the American Express package's mysterious arrival, but most of all, that undeniable sense of healing and hope and, yes, forgiveness. Her awareness became a bright light. "I had been given a miracle, and I had missed it!" Kelley says. But she would not miss another.

Today Kelley is a college graduate, the mother of a young son, and a confident, faith-filled woman, at peace with herself and with God. "God does the divine stuff, and I do the legwork," she says. "I don't worry about anything. I always feel safe because if I'm doing what I'm supposed to, then he will take care of the rest."

She likes to think that Peter McGucky is happy about her change of heart, and will tell her so when they meet again.

What Do the Children Know?

Little ones to Him belong,
They are weak but He is strong.
—"Jesus Loves Me," hymn

Because they are so innocent, small children accept even the most improbable things as perfectly normal. Perhaps they are in touch with heaven in a way we can only imagine.

Johnnie and William Edwards, of Athens, Georgia, had been married for ten years before they conceived a child. During her pregnancy, Johnnie fell on her stomach, was in an automobile accident, and, a month from delivery, suffered complications and had to be induced. "Given all this, when I held my perfect baby boy, Demetrius, in my arms, I felt he was a miracle child," Johnnie says.

Johnnie delighted in motherhood, but it was not without anxieties. There was so much to learn, and each time Demetrius tried something new, Johnnie felt apprehensive. When he turned three and his day care center offered swimming lessons at the YMCA, she had mixed emotions. She certainly wanted him to learn to swim. But what if something happened? Reluctantly she enrolled him. "But on the days of swim class I worried constantly, until he was safely home," she says.

About this time, Johnnie purchased a child's Bible for Demetrius. They hadn't talked about spiritual things yet, so she decided to read him one story each night as a beginning. That evening Johnnie tucked Demetrius into bed, picked up the new Bible, and turned to the story of Jacob and the angel. Her little son's eyes lit up.

"Mommy!" he cried, pointing to the picture of the winged being. "I saw this lady today!"

"You did?" Johnnie asked, astonished.

"Uh-huh. In the pool!"

Demetrius was a very truthful little boy. And yet children *did* have fantasies. "This is an angel, honey," Johnnie explained carefully. "Did anyone else see her, maybe your teacher?"

"I don't think so," Demetrius answered.

"Did she say anything to you?"

"No, she just smiled at me and stood near me and held my hand. After my head went underwater when it wasn't supposed to." He looked thoughtful. "I think she came because I was a little scared."

Tears pricked Johnnie's eyes. *She* had been a little scared, too. But now she knew God had his hand on her child, and there was no need to worry about water—or anything else.

Little ones' special visions aren't limited to angels. Brad, the baby son of Peter and Darlene Kutulas, was just learning to talk and knew only a few words. One was "Dada." "Dada" was not reserved for his father, however; when Brad saw *any* man, he would shriek "Dada!" in delight. In an effort to encourage him to talk more, Darlene and Peter often showed him photographs of people in magazines. Brad would always point to the man. "Dada!"

One afternoon Peter said to Darlene, "Let's show Brad a picture of Jesus." The baby had never seen one, and given the long hair and flowing robes, they wondered how he would categorize Jesus. But when they held the picture up, Brad suddenly grew solemn, pointed almost in recognition, and said—again and again—a word he had never used: "King!"

Some little ones seem to be spiritually aware, even when such ideas are never discussed in the home. One self-described agnostic mother reported that her two-year-old, Joey, talked constantly with his imaginary companion, Mr. Bones, who was "all dressed in white." She attempted to humor Joey, by pretending that his "friend" really existed.

"Where did Mr. Bones come from?" she once asked her son.

Joey looked at her seriously. "I knew him in heaven," he said.

By the time Elizabeth Cockrell was eighteen months old, she could identify several colors and talk clearly and constantly. Her mother, Cynthia, would hear her chattering away while playing in her room. One day Cynthia stuck her head in the bedroom door. "Whom are you talking to, Elizabeth?" she asked, smiling.

Elizabeth looked up, with wide innocent eyes. "Little Billy," she answered.

Cynthia felt a chill. "Who?"

"Him name Little Billy, Mommy, and him's a boy." Elizabeth was sure.

"What does he look like, honey?"

Cynthia is part Cherokee, and her daughters have inherited her dark hair. But instead of choosing a doll with a family resemblance, Elizabeth paused, looked around the room, and spotted a blond doll. "Him hair like *that*," she said, pointing, "and him eyes blue."

Cynthia was ready to weep. "Why do you call him Little Billy, Elizabeth?" she asked gently.

"Him *say* his name is Little Billy," Elizabeth explained. It seemed reasonable to her.

But Cynthia went to the kitchen, sat down at the table, and put her head in her hands. One week before Elizabeth was born, Cynthia's cousin's baby boy had died of sudden infant death syndrome. He had been four months old, with blond hair and blue eyes, and from the moment of his birth, the family had dubbed him Little Billy. "My cousin lives in a different state, and we never discussed the tragedy," Cynthia said. "So how could Elizabeth have heard about it?"

Cynthia never again asked her daughter about Little Billy. But for the next few years, Elizabeth always insisted that he was right by her side.

Children occasionally report out-of-body experiences. In *Parting Visions*, author Melvin Morse tells of six-year-old Ann, who had leukemia and had been feeling very sick. After she had gone to bed one evening, Ann saw a glowing form in her room, which turned into a beautiful lady. "We moved through darkness into an incredibly bright and colorful world, like nothing I had ever seen," Ann later explained. "The lady said that I needed a rest, that life was very hard for me."

Enjoying the unaccustomed feeling of peace and joy, Ann played for a while with other children in a sandbox. Then, guided by the lady, she returned to her room, waved good-bye to the lady, and fell asleep. Within two weeks, all Ann's blood tests had returned to normal, and the leukemia was gone.[4]

Although she was not ill like Ann, four-year-old Sarah Richter of Kansas City, Missouri, had a similar story to tell her mother one morning. "I saw Jesus in my room last night!" she said, full of innocence and excitement.

"Really? What did he look like?" Rita asked, smiling.

"Like a bright light. He didn't say much, but he took me up to heaven with him."

Rita's smile faded. She hadn't taken Sarah to church very often, and the child didn't know very much about Jesus. Why would Sarah describe him as a "light"? "Tell me about heaven," Rita said.

"It's a great place for kids, Mom," Sarah answered. "It has suckers and playhouses. Jesus sat on a cloud and watched me play. Then he said it was time to go home."

"Did you?"

"Yes. He stayed in my room and held me for a little while," Sarah said. "Then he went back to heaven."

A few years have passed, and Sarah's experience hasn't happened again. But sometimes, when she's afraid of the dark, "she says she knows Jesus is holding her, and she falls asleep quickly," Rita reports. Her daughter's faith has touched her heart.

A caller phoned radio station KRLD in Dallas one evening when the host and I were discussing children's spiritual insights.

"Bobby, our only child, was almost three when my wife had an early miscarriage," the caller told listeners. "Because she had to stay overnight in the hospital, I brought Bobby to see her that evening. We hadn't told anyone about the pregnancy or loss. Bobby knew only that Mommy was sick."

The moment Bobby entered his mother's hospital room, he climbed up on her bed and looked at her with tender concern. "Don't be sad, Mommy." He patted her cheek gently. "In one year, you're going to have another baby."

Shocked, the couple looked at each other. How could Bobby have known about the situation? "He would never answer any questions," Bobby's father explained. "But one year later—to the exact date—my wife gave birth to a healthy daughter."

William Coughlin had been ill for a long time, and his six adult offspring were saddened but not surprised when their mother called them to his bedside for the last time. Slowly they gathered, bringing their spouses and children. Some of the older children were a bit hesitant to hug Grandpa, but four-year-old Erin Murphy had no such inhibitions. "Oh, Papa, I love you so much!" she declared as she threw her arms around him.

During William's last hours, after the grandchildren had been tucked into bed, his family sang songs—"On Eagles' Wings," and

"Be Not Afraid"—and quietly said good-bye. As William died, serenity filled the room. Despite their grief, everyone knew he had found peace and rest.

The following morning Peggy Murphy went to break the news to her three small daughters, who had fallen asleep on the family room floor. "I have something to tell you," she began gently as they awakened.

But Erin had news, too. "You don't have to tell me, Mom. I already know," she said. "Papa went to heaven last night."

"That's right." Peggy nodded. "But how did you know?"

Erin seemed surprised that anyone would ask. "I saw him leaving," she said simply. "He didn't look at me, but he went right by. He was smiling and happy."

Smiling and happy. How Peggy wanted to believe it! "Was he alone?" she asked.

Erin pointed to a picture of Jesus in the kitchen. "No. Papa was with *him*. They flew out the patio doors together."

For the Coughlin family, it was a final gift. As so often happens, a little child had led them.

God Knows Where We Are

Suppose you plant a garden, and after a few days, you don't see results.
Do you dig it up again? No, because you know that a lot of things are
going on that you can't see. It's the same with God.

—Dr. Charles Stanley, pastor, First Baptist Church, Atlanta, Georgia

When Art Cooney was ordained a Capuchin friar in 1976, he was fully prepared for the life of a missionary. He would travel wherever he was sent, happy to preach the word of God to those hungry for hope. He did go to several countries, and enjoyed his work very much. Then, while living temporarily in Saginaw, Michigan, he met Marge Fobear and Nancy Kawiecki at a charismatic prayer meeting. The women had a healing ministry and frequently laid hands on those who were sick. The three began praying together to support each other's work.

Eventually Father Art was assigned to a mission post in Nicaragua. Marge and Nancy assured him they would pray for him on a regular basis while he was there. Other friends and relatives promised mail and care packages. His mother gave him a card that read, "The will of God will never lead you where the grace of God cannot find you."

But when Father Art arrived at his new station, he soon forgot this comforting send-off, for this part of Nicaragua was extremely primitive. The only paved road ended in his town, named *Muelle de los Bueyes*—literally, "place where the oxen cross." And they did. "Everything looked straight out of the old West," Father recalls. "Farmers and ranchers rode into town on horseback, some carrying six-guns. There were gunfights in front of the saloon and cattle drives through town. I thought I had gone back in time a hundred years."

More discouraging was the food—most often rice and beans. Mixed together, it was called *gallopinto*, but Father wasn't fooled. After a few weeks he began dreaming of hamburgers.

Time passed, and no mail arrived from home. And although the Nicaraguans were warm and friendly, Father began to feel forsaken. Why had he gotten stuck in this primitive place? Where was all that support his friends had pledged? Social isolation was difficult, but far more wretched was his growing spiritual loneliness. He had never felt abandoned by God, but now "it seemed as if God had dropped me in the middle of the jungle, and forgotten about me." He often read the message on the prayer card his mother had given him. Where was that promised grace now?

Despite Father Art's misery, there was work to be done. His new parish comprised forty rural communities, most accessible only by horse or mule, so he planned a ten-day mission trip to several of them. Packing only what he and his guides could fit into saddlebags, and wrapping his clothes in plastic to keep them dry in tropical downpours, he set out. He and his guides visited several small villages, bathing in the rivers and holding evening services by lantern light. It was what he had been sent to do, and it could have been adventurous, even fun. But Father's heart was heavy. He still had not received any letters from home. And God seemed as distant as ever.

Then, on the fifth or sixth day on the jungle trail, Father's horse abruptly spooked and bucked. Father clung to the saddle, but the animal crashed to the ground, trapping him underneath. "My left leg was pinned under the horse and my left foot was caught in the stirrup," he said. "I couldn't free myself, and I began to panic as the horse started to roll back and forth on me, trying to right itself." If the horse got to its feet, it would take off running, he knew, dragging him behind. He would be pulled into trees and die, or at the least, be seriously injured. There were no doctors in this isolated place—who could care for him? "Lord!" he shouted. "Help me!"

Instantly a deep and profound peace settled around him like a warm blanket. Why, God was with him, right here in this unlikely place! He knew it! And he would be all right, despite the thrashing animal still on top of him. "Further, I was suddenly aware that I hadn't been abandoned by anyone, ever," he says. "There were people praying for me, many people, and I *felt* that support."

By now, the guides were working to calm the horse. Gradually they did so, and pulled Father to his feet. He brushed himself off, gingerly feeling his arms and especially his legs. Amazingly, neither he nor the horse was hurt. All was well, just as he had sensed.

Father finished his trip and returned to his work at *Muelle de los Bueyes* with a far lighter heart. But it was a few weeks before he realized the full significance of that moment of grace in the jungle. A letter finally arrived, from his prayer warriors, Marge and Nancy, relating a strange story.

"We were on our way to the hospital to pray with a sick friend," Marge wrote. "We had just pulled into a parking space when Nancy felt a sharp pain in her left leg near her thigh. It was so intense that, when she opened the car door, she could not stand or get out. Nothing like this had ever happened to her."

The women began to pray in tongues. But as they continued, a strange feeling came over Nancy.

"This isn't about me," she told Marge. "I think it's Art. He's in some kind of trouble."

The two continued to pray—now for Father Art—for about five minutes. Abruptly Nancy's pain left her, and the women went on to visit their friend.

Now Marge had some questions. "What happened to you?" she wrote. "And how is your leg?"

A lump was forming in Father Art's throat as he looked at his calendar. For the women's prayers in the parking lot perfectly matched the day, the exact *moment*, of his accident in the jungle, half a world away.

"It is hard to describe how much that letter meant to me, and how it strengthened my faith," Father Art says. God did indeed know where each of his children was, and his grace was ample for their needs. The prayer card had been right.

DREAM MAKER

God has chosen her as a pattern for the other angels.

—EPITAPH IN AN ENGLISH CHURCHYARD

Not everyone knows what a good true friend is all about," says Joni Loughran, of Petaluma, California. But she does. It was in sophomore year of high school that she and redheaded Patty McNamara met in geometry class and experienced that instant and special bond that's hard to describe, but so meaningful when it occurs.

Patty was a "people person," vibrant, outgoing, and beloved by many, with indulgent parents and an adoring older brother, Rich. Joni, by contrast, was withdrawn, contemplative, and shy. "Patty held a very unique place in my heart because I felt totally comfortable with her right away," Joni explains. "She accepted me without judgment. I can't remember her ever hurting my feelings." One night, as the girls reflected on their relationship, they talked about how difficult life would be without each other. "We even said that if something happened to one of us, the other would follow," Joni recalls. "It was a poignant moment, especially for two teenagers."

The girls stayed in close touch as they matured, although Patty eventually moved away. When they were twenty-three, Joni got married in a quick ceremony with just her family present. She was looking forward to telling Patty all about it in a long, satisfying cross-country phone call just as soon as life got back to normal. But a week after the wedding, Patty's brother, Rich, called. "Joni, I've got terrible news . . . ," Rich began. He sounded numb, as if he were under anesthesia.

"What's happened, Rich?"

"It's Patty. She . . . Tonight she was sitting in the back of a pickup truck, coming home from a county fair with friends, holding a teddy bear her boyfriend had won for her." The truck had bounced into a shallow ditch, and Patty had flipped out, hitting her head on a rock. "She's been here in the emergency room in a coma, but—" A sob racked Rich. "Joni, she just died."

Joni clung to the phone in disbelief. It couldn't be! Not Patty! But Rich's anguish spelled certainty. As tears spilled down her cheeks, Joni felt a part of herself dying, too.

The following weeks were torture. Unable to express herself easily to people, Joni grieved silently, her heart completely torn in two. Her new husband couldn't grasp the magnitude of her loss, and suggested that she "get over it."

"Because of this lack of support, the burden was mine alone," Joni says, "but I was in denial. I didn't go to the funeral, and stupid as it sounds, for a while I pretended she did not die. I was quite inept at coping with her loss."

Weeks dragged by, and Joni became even more depressed. She felt convinced that since she and Patty had vowed to stay together, something was bound to happen to her, too, perhaps a car crash or a terrible illness. Lonely and heartbroken, she waited for the end.

One day several weeks after Patty's accident, Joni awakened with a sense of something lingering. She had been dreaming, and somehow she knew it had been an *important* dream. Patty had not been there, but a messenger had spoken to her in the dream, telling her something quite significant. Joni tried to remember as she headed down the hallway, but it was like grasping cloud fragments. Then she stopped, as if she had been hit gently over the head.

"I suddenly remembered the entire dream, in every detail," Joni says. "An angel had come, telling me very clearly that Patty wanted me to know that she was all right. I would see her in due time, but I was not to go with her now." Joni needed to stay in this world, the messenger had explained, because she was newly pregnant and had to raise her son.

Pregnant! Joni hadn't considered the possibility. And the angel had delivered the news with great joy, with the inference that Patty was very happy about it.

But what did a dream *really* mean? Joni asked herself as she headed off to a class she was taking. Weren't dreams just fantasies, or leftover meaningless pieces of the day? And if Patty was truly sending her a message from heaven, why hadn't God sent *her* instead of an angel? Yet Joni recalled the sense of deep spiritual conviction that had come upon her as she stood in the hallway, the feeling that she could trust the angel's words.

That night Joni fell asleep easily, and in the middle of the night, the dream came again. But this time Patty herself stood before Joni. She seemed radiant, elated, aware of Joni's ongoing grief, yet—now that Joni understood she was to stay on earth—ready to console her. "It's okay," Patty said. "I know you're sad, Joni, but you don't have to be. Everything is fine with me. And you're going to be a mother!"

"But I miss you so much." Joni felt like crying again.

Patty smiled. "From now on, whenever you need to see me, just meet me in your dreams."

In her dreams. The vision was fading now, and Joni awakened. Was this possible? Was any of it real, and not just an invention of her exhausted mind?

A few days later, Joni visited her physician. She was indeed expecting a child, the surprised doctor told her, even though as yet she had experienced no pregnancy symptoms. Almost exactly nine months later, her son Travis was born.

"I wish that Patty had not left so soon, and I still miss her, although twenty years have passed," Joni says today. But dreams of her continue, not necessarily "on cue," but frequently enough for Joni to know that she and Patty are still connected, and that healing has indeed taken place.

"My current dreams are never about Patty and me missing each other," she says. "They are mostly integrated in my present life situations, such as Patty being at my son's graduation or Patty seeing my new home. Occasionally the dreams take us back to our teen years, and we relive an event. The dreams change their focus, but of course, Patty looks the same. She has not aged."

Patty promised that she and Joni would meet in Joni's dreams, and she has kept that promise. How? Joni is not sure. "I suspect the desire or need for these meetings is born somewhere other than my conscious mind," she muses. "It's a place that responds to a longing in the heart and transcends time and space, a harbor for a rendezvous of the spirits." A place, she thinks, very much like heaven.

Erin's Christmas Vision

*Defend, O Lord, this child with thy heavenly grace, that (s)he may
continue thine forever.*

—Book of Common Prayer

Kathy and Mike Felke, of northwest suburban Illinois, were
thrilled at the birth of their second daughter, Erin, in 1978.
But unlike her older sister, Kate, Erin seemed fragile. Although she
walked early, she preferred being carried. "Everyone thought she was
an exceptionally good baby because she always sat in my lap, and
she slept a lot," says Kathy, a registered dental hygienist. "Actually,
she caught every illness that came around, especially ear infections.
I knew enough about health to realize something was wrong."

Kathy and Mike repeatedly mentioned their concern about Erin
to their pediatrician. But blood tests showed nothing. Finally the
doctor told Kathy that she was just "an overly concerned mother."

On December 23, 1980, two-year-old Erin seemed unusually list-
less. She barely ate breakfast, then fell asleep on the couch. Kathy

looked at her. "I could almost see the veins under her skin," she says, "and the shadows around her eyes were as dark as her hair." Kathy phoned her pediatrician's partner and insisted on an immediate appointment.

The new doctor checked Erin. "How long has she looked like this?" he asked abruptly.

Kathy thought. "Over a year. But tests haven't shown anything."

"I want a complete blood workup at the hospital," he said, reaching for the phone. "Bring her there right now."

Kathy did. The following morning, Christmas Eve, the physician phoned. "I have some bad news," he told her. "Erin is gravely ill. It might be aplastic anemia or leukemia."

Kathy's heart seemed to stop.

"I've arranged for a private room at Loyola Medical Center," the doctor went on. "The chief of hematology there will take over Erin's treatment. You can take her in early on the twenty-sixth." He stopped, then sighed. "She might as well spend Christmas at home."

Kathy didn't miss the tinge of hopelessness in his voice. Devastated, she told Mike, then began phoning family members.

The following morning Kathy bravely dressed Erin in her red jumper, onto which Erin's grandmother pinned a little gold angel pin. They reached Holy Ghost Parish in Wood Dale, and went to the sanctuary where Father Tom White was vesting, to tell him what had happened.

Father White listened. He blessed Erin and added her name to the list of ill parishioners who would be prayed for during Christmas Mass. And, although the Felkes hadn't realized it yet, he threw away his prepared homily. "I do that a lot," Father White says today. "Sometimes everything I planned to say will change in an instant."

A few moments later, Father White stood in front of a packed church. Looking down, he saw Erin in the front row, drowsing on Kathy's lap.

"Life isn't easy," he began. "Sometimes we're presented with things we can't accept, situations too big to even comprehend. And we get mad at God about it." He began to pace back and forth in front of the congregation. "During those times, God understands how we feel—and it's okay to be angry with him. But we also have to remember that we don't need to just lie down and take it." Father White looked at the Felkes in the first row. "No—when we're presented with heartbreak, he wants us to *fight*! We have to use the faith we've been given!"

On the way home from church, Kathy and Mike agreed that the priest had given them hope. Tomorrow the battle would begin.

The next morning, Kathy packed Erin's crib sheet, potty-chair, special dish, and drawings from Kate to hang near her bed. "Maybe I was in denial, but I wanted everything to be as normal and familiar as possible," she says. A team of physicians met them at the hospital, and when they found that Erin's hemoglobin had sunk to

4.5 (a normal reading is between 11 and 15), the pace quickened. A bone marrow test revealed that Erin's body was making red cells, yet something was destroying them almost immediately. But what?

Kathy and Mike gave extensive family histories. Specialists examined everything for clues—their use of pesticides, their allergies, the antibiotics used to combat Erin's constant ear infections. And everything led to a dead end. Three days later there was still no diagnosis, no recommended treatment.

Kathy refused to go home, so nurses brought a bed for her. "At one point a nurse told me that a prayer group had assembled in the playroom and wanted to see me," she said. Kathy went out to meet them. "They said they had heard about Erin and had come to pray for her, but they didn't introduce themselves, and I had never seen any of them before." The group knelt in a circle, with Kathy in their midst, and prayed strongly for healing. They were fighting, Kathy realized, fighting for a toddler they had never met. But being away from Erin upset her, and she didn't stay long. The next time she left Erin's side, the group had gone.

By the evening of the twenty-eighth, Erin was sleeping almost constantly. When the doctor came, he shook his head. "You'd better prepare yourself," he told Kathy gently. "We're losing her. The only possibility left is a blood transfusion, to keep her alive a little longer. But we can't find a compatible donor right now."

"Take mine!" But Kathy already knew she wasn't a match.

"Look, Mrs. Felke," the doctor continued, "Erin's oxygen level is falling. So I think you need to face—"

"No!" She couldn't! The doctor quietly left. At midnight a priest appeared, prayed over Erin, and anointed her. They were all fighting for Erin, Kathy realized: Mike, at home with Kate, Father White, the hospital staff, all the people who were praying. She might be lonely, but she and Erin were not alone. Intently she watched her daughter. *Fight, Erin, fight.* Every breath, every heartbeat, was a small victory.

But Erin's skin was almost transparent now, her eyes ringed with shadows. A haze seemed to be lying over her, as if life was ebbing away, growing fainter, foggier.

Suddenly, at 1:30 a.m., Erin opened her eyes. She looked aware, *present.* Kathy was astonished. "Lights, Mommy. Lights!" Erin whispered, her gaze fixed on something above Kathy's head. Kathy turned but saw nothing in the darkened room.

"Where are the lights, honey?" she whispered, turning back. "What do you see?"

Erin looked thrilled. "Bells, Mommy!" she cried, her voice slightly stronger. "Lights and bells!"

The hospital corridors were completely hushed. Kathy's skin prickled. What could Erin be hearing? Was she hallucinating? No, she seemed extremely alert.

Now Erin smiled. Raising a tiny hand, she pointed to the corner of the room. "Pretty ladies, Mommy. See them?" On her face was an expression of joy.

Pretty ladies. Kathy was afraid to turn around. What would she see? She had heard that angels came to carry people home to heaven. Was that what was happening? Was Erin seeing angels?

No! Suddenly Kathy's heart seemed to break. She hadn't fought yet, she realized—others had been doing it for her. But now it was her turn! *Oh God, angels, don't take her!* she prayed silently. *Take me—not her. She hasn't even started to live. Please, please.*

A nurse came into the room. "We've found a reasonable blood match," she told Kathy. "We're going to start a very slow transfusion. You'll have to watch each drop, in case it begins to clot."

Kathy looked back at Erin. Her daughter's eyes were closing again. But a smile remained on her lips.

Kathy stayed alert for the rest of the night, watching the miniature droplets inch down the tube and into her daughter. Would the transfusion work? If not, Kathy knew, there were no other options.

Mike came in early that morning, while Erin was still sleeping. So he, too, witnessed the beginning of the miracle. "She awakened, and we both just stared at her," Kathy says. There was color in her daughter's lips. Erin's cheeks were pink, not gray.

"Do you feel like breakfast?" Kathy asked.

Erin nodded.

By evening, her hemoglobin had mysteriously increased to eight. "We don't know what has happened," her physician told the Felkes. "But the transfusion must have worked, because Erin seems fine. She might as well go home now."

Erin's symptoms never returned. Because she left the hospital with her condition still described as "undiagnosed," Kathy and Mike were not aware of what had actually happened to Erin until several years later.

"When we moved and changed doctors, I brought Erin's records to our new pediatrician," Kathy says. "He was interested, and did some research." Only then did she learn, says Kathy, that Erin's disease was a rare form of anemia, one that at that time had proved fatal to six of the only seven Americans who'd been diagnosed with it. There had been no treatment then, and although blood transfusions had been tried in other cases, they had never worked.

Today Erin enjoys a rich and healthy life. She has earned a PhD in physical therapy, is on the staff at Johns Hopkins Medical Center, and travels all over the world in her "spare" time.

Kathy's learned much from this difficult episode, especially about God and the power of prayer. "I don't know why he healed Erin and not another child whose parents loved her just as much and prayed just as hard," she says. "But I know now that it's okay to be mad at him. He doesn't hold grudges, and he does understand." And when his light breaks through our darkness, Kathy knows, it can conquer even death itself.

Heavenly Sights

We carry within us the wonders we seek without us.

—Sir Thomas Browne, *Religio Medici*

In today's climate of signs and wonders, visions are especially interesting. Two types that occurred in biblical days are frequently reported now as well. One is an *inner* vision, a scene or event perceived with the eyes of the spirit rather than with physical eyes. The other is an actual apparition, when the supernatural temporarily intrudes into everyday life for reasons perhaps only God knows.

Diane Alfred of Tallahassee, Florida, experienced a vision while praying one Sunday in church. Without any warning, "an image of my son Jeremy flashed before my eyes," she says. "He was in his car, racing down a long two-lane Georgia road. Other cars appeared in this scene, and I was overcome with fear." Diane began to pray intensely: "God, protect my son. God, protect my son." She was certain Jeremy was in extreme danger.

Suddenly Diane felt as if she were flying through the air. Now she was hovering over Jeremy's car, now passing through the roof. She saw her son behind the wheel as feathered wings wrapped him in a soft embrace. Diane looked to the right, where Jeremy's girlfriend sat. She watched as one of the wings reached over to embrace the girl as well. "It was almost as if I was *inside* the angel, looking at the scene through her eyes," she says. Then Diane heard the squeal of tires, the crash of metal, screams.

Slowly the scene receded, and she realized she was still in church, still pleading, praying on her knees while everyone else was standing up. How could she have lost contact with her surroundings, felt as if she had actually been transported through space? Diane stood up, shaky and confused.

Later, at home, she was still puzzling over the episode. Should she try to reach Jeremy? Suddenly the phone rang. It was her older son, Jason. "Mom," he said, "don't get excited. Everyone's okay. But Jeremy and his girlfriend were in a bad car wreck this morning. It was on a busy two-lane highway in Georgia."

Diane gripped the telephone. "What time did it happen?" she asked.

But she already knew. The accident had occurred at the very moment she'd received the vision of her son. Her prayers had somehow summoned the angel who protected him and his passenger.

Dr. Candace Williamson Murdock of Rome, Georgia, had just had a miscarriage. The night after she returned from the hospital, she stayed awake, restless and upset. This baby had not been her first, but like all children, it was irreplaceable, and she grieved deeply at its loss. "Suddenly a scene appeared—as if it was on a movie screen—right in front of me," Candace recounts. She blinked, but the vision remained.

It was a sunny green meadow. In its midst were dogs playing and chasing each other, moving toward the right side. "The dogs seemed somehow familiar," she says. "I suddenly realized that they were our family pets, dogs from my childhood!" Watching intently, Candace then saw her father running into the center of the scene, the dogs leaping joyfully about him. Her father had been killed in a plane crash seven years ago. He had raised, and always loved, dogs.

Then Candace realized that her father was not alone. He was gripping the hand of a small blond child. They were looking toward the right. Candace's father seemed to be pointing at something, as if he were explaining it—and both were smiling. Instantly Candace knew this child was the baby she'd just lost. Obviously her father was welcoming the child into heaven, and God had allowed her to witness it so she would be consoled.

"I cannot explain how much comfort this vision gave me," Candace says. "I had never experienced anything like it, nor would I have pictured heaven in this way, but I was *not* hallucinating. To know that my child, my father, and his beloved dogs were all together was the best answer to prayer that I could have asked for. God does care."

The Right Reverend Robert R. Shahan, bishop of the Episcopal Diocese of Arizona, recalls when he and others were interviewing priests for a church position. Each applicant was asked to describe the most profound spiritual experience he had ever had. One story, says Bishop Shahan, was especially hard to forget.

The church was filled that Sunday morning, and the priest had just ascended the pulpit to begin his sermon. Casually he looked up at the beautiful vaulted ceiling, and his heart seemed to stop. Far above the congregation, in a corner over the choir loft, floated two huge angels, clothed in white.

Father gasped, then recovered smoothly—years of training before an audience had served him well. But—was something actually *there*? Unobtrusively he looked up again. Yes! Magnificent creatures, glorious and glowing, one with his hands raised in an attitude of blessing over the congregation.

But it couldn't be. Why would angels grace *his* church? He was just an ordinary person. Quickly, Father brought his gaze back to his prepared text. He must be hallucinating, he thought, for the congregation was as quiet and attentive as ever. Surely if something was actually *up there*, someone else would see it, too. And apparently no one had.

He needed a vacation. That was it. He would get through this service as quickly as possible, then phone his bishop to ask for time off to rest and recover. He hurried to his homily's close, then returned to the altar. The next time he peeked at the ceiling, the figures had disappeared.

The service seemed interminable, but as it ended, Father's heart rate had almost returned to normal, and he walked calmly to the back of the church to greet the congregation. His flock filed past, unusually talkative and vibrant.

"What a lovely service, Father!"

"Church seemed especially interesting today."

The comments were warm, encouraging. If only they knew, these dear people who put so much faith in his leadership.

The end of the line was in sight, and finally one elderly lady was left. She stepped up and took his hand. "You seemed a bit distracted today, Father, at the beginning of your homily," she said.

"Well, yes." He smiled. "But it was nothing, really."

"Oh, but I think it was." The woman bent toward him. The air around them seemed charged with electricity, as if they were alone in a circle of love. Then she beamed and lowered her voice. "You saw them, too, didn't you?" she said.

Joan Clayton of Portales, New Mexico, was concerned about the girl her son Lane was going to marry. The young couple seemed to argue constantly. A little incompatibility was normal in any relationship, Joan mused as she and her husband drove home from a weekend at Lane's college campus. But her son and future daughter-in-law disagreed on *everything*, and always had, right from the beginning of their relationship. Now Joan leaned back and closed her eyes. *Lord,* she prayed silently, *if this is not the right girl for Lane, please send the right one into his life.*

Immediately Joan experienced a vivid inner vision of two girls. Although the one on the left was only a darkened silhouette, Joan recognized her as Lane's fiancée. The smiling girl on the right, however, Joan had never seen before. She was a beautiful blue-eyed blonde, dazzling and vivacious—in living color.

The scene lasted briefly, but long enough for Joan to know it had not just been her imagination. "There is something that happens in your spirit, perhaps an awareness of God's timing. It's hard to explain, but you know that this is not an ordinary experience," Joan says.

During the following months, Joan occasionally thought of the vision and wondered what it meant. Surely she shouldn't take it seriously, especially since her son's wedding plans were in full swing. Two weeks before the big event, however, Lane's fiancée called off the wedding. Lane was devastated.

Two years later, the Claytons went to Lane's campus to attend his college graduation. "When we arrived at his apartment, he asked us to wait while he went to pick up a friend," Joan says. When Lane returned with his friend Kari, Joan gasped. It was the blue-eyed blond girl she had seen in her vision two years earlier.

Today Kari is Joan's daughter-in-law and the mother of her grandchildren. "She is the most wonderful girl in the whole world," says Joan, "and everyone who knows her agrees that she came straight from the Lord."

Vallorie Neal had been brought up in a lovely home by parents who worked hard to support their large family. But she married Wayne Wood against her parents' wishes—they did not feel Wayne could provide well for Vallorie—and though she and Wayne had a wonderful relationship, her parents became somewhat estranged from them. Occasionally they would show up at unexpected moments to check on their daughter's well-being, then they would retreat into quiet disapproval. Now Vallorie and Wayne had hit difficult financial times, and they were being evicted.

"Our second baby was only two months old, and I probably could have gone to my parents and asked for help," Vallorie recalls. "But I couldn't bring myself to do it because I knew they would think our marriage was a failure." Instead, she and Wayne borrowed one hundred dollars to put their furniture in storage, and slept in their car at a truck stop, praying all the while that Wayne would find a job.

On the third day, Wayne applied for emergency aid, and that evening he received enough to pay for a room at the Miron Motel. Vallorie was relieved that her family would sleep in beds that night, but she still worried about not keeping in touch with her folks. At midnight she finally turned off the light. "God," she murmured into the darkness. "I need some help. I don't know how you'll do it, but could you please let Mom and Dad know that I'm okay?"

Early the following morning, Vallorie and Wayne took the babies and went out to get some coffee. "We didn't have enough money for breakfast," Vallorie recalls. When they returned, there was a note on their motel room door. "Call me. Mother," it said.

Vallorie started to tremble. It was definitely her mother's handwriting. But how had Mrs. Neal known where to find them, and particularly their specific room, number 25? When Vallorie phoned, however, she realized how tenderly God had answered her prayer of the previous night.

Mrs. Neal explained that she had paid an unexpected visit to Vallorie's apartment earlier that week, only to learn from neighbors that the Woods had just been evicted. For the next few days she had waited for a phone call from her daughter, but when Vallorie hadn't contacted her, Mrs. Neal had become increasingly concerned. Where could the young family be? Were they safe? Did they have food, shelter? By the third evening, her worry was overwhelming her, and she had to take a risk. "Mark," she told Vallorie's younger brother, "please drive around town and see if you can find Vallorie and Wayne's car."

Mark had been gone several hours, and Mrs. Neal was in bed when she heard the front door open. She looked at the clock: 1:00 a.m. Had he found his sister? All the lights came on through the house, and Mark came in and stood at the foot of her bed. There seemed to be another man standing at the bedroom door, although she could not see him clearly. Perhaps a friend of Mark's?

"Vallorie is in room 25 at the Miron Motel," Mark announced. He did not mention his companion, or provide any additional details.

It didn't matter. Her daughter was safe—if only temporarily. "Thanks, Mark," Vallorie's mother said, relieved. "You go on to bed." Tomorrow she would decide what to do.

Mrs. Neal fell asleep quickly. However, she awakened when the front door slammed. Her bedside clock said 4:00 a.m. Who? Again the lights came on throughout the house, and Mark strode into her room. "I found Vallorie," he said. "I don't know what room she's staying in, but her car is parked at the Miron Motel."

Puzzled, Mrs. Neal sat up. "Mark, why did you wake me? You and your friend told me hours ago that Vallorie is in room 25 at the Miron."

"No I didn't," Mark protested. "I've been looking for her all night—I just got here. And I've been alone the whole time."

The Neals eventually grew to love their son-in-law. And Vallorie and Wayne have a wonderful and fulfilling life today in Lithia Springs, Georgia. But the family still marvels over Mrs. Neal's vision. Who visited her that night, just an hour after her daughter's prayer, with the specific information she needed? Who was standing in the shadows, watching the scene? No one knows for sure, but Vallorie learned a valuable lesson. "During those hard times, I thought God had forgotten me," she says. "But he knew where I was all along."

NOTHING AT ALL TOO SMALL

Prayer is a cry of distress, a demand for help, a hymn of love.

—Dr. Alexis Carrel, French surgeon

On a cold Sunday afternoon a few years ago, David Miller, age thirteen, and his ten-year-old brother, Nicholas, decided to go sledding on a hill just a short distance from their home in South Sioux City, Nebraska. The hill was covered with six inches of new snow, and trails had been cut into it by earlier sledders, making it especially fun. The boys and their friends were having a wonderful time, and then disaster struck. Whizzing downhill, David's sled hit a bump. "Oh no!" he shouted as he tried to brake. "My glasses just flew off!"

"Uh-oh." Nicholas didn't wear glasses, but he knew how important they were. He and David would have to find them right away, before they were trampled by the other kids or buried until spring!

The boys searched for almost an hour, going up and down the hill on each side of the many sled trails, even looking on the edges near the highway and in the tall broom grass that poked above the drifts. They found nothing. Finally, as dusk approached, they trudged home and reported the loss to their father, Dave.

Dave is something of an optimist. A deacon in the South Sioux Assembly of God church, he's a husband and father of four, and considers himself a fortunate man. Although the sun was already down, he thought he and the boys should look again. Surely the glasses would turn up.

The three headed back to the hill. But by now, young David no longer remembered which trail he had been sledding on, or whether his glasses had flown off nearer the top or the bottom of the hill. "I began to realize that there had been hordes of kids playing here all day, and probably someone had accidentally crushed them underfoot already," Dave said. As darkness fell, they gave up. But Dave decided to try again the next morning. He would use his metal detector, one of his favorite hobby items. "Although," he says, "it doesn't get much of a workout in the snow."

But the next morning, the Miller family awakened to the worst of all scenarios. Two inches of new snow had fallen during the night. "I like a challenge," Dave says, "but this was certainly like looking for the proverbial needle in the haystack." Still, he took a rake and his metal detector and went back to the hill. Before starting his painstaking task, he remembered to check the batteries in the metal detector. They were dead. How could that be? He had just replaced them this morning.

Sighing, Dave laid down the useless machine and began to rake. It was his only option. Inch by painstaking inch, he worked his way up the first sled trail. His toes froze. People driving by gave him strange looks. He started on the second trail, but he wasn't getting anywhere.

This was stupid. It was impossible. He would have to give up. Suddenly Dave heard a little voice inside him. "Did you ever think to *pray?*" the voice chided him gently. "Did you ever consider asking God to find the glasses?" Dave felt humbled and embarrassed all at the same time. He, a deacon at his church, had been so headstrong, so *in charge*, that he hadn't even thought to begin at the beginning! Without a thought for the drivers who would see him as they passed, Dave knelt down in the snow, folded his hands, and closed his eyes.

"God, I'm sorry that I forgot about you," he whispered. "I try never to do that, not for a minute. Please forgive me now. And please find the glasses." He stayed silent a moment longer, then opened his eyes.

In front of him lay David's glasses. Despite last night's snowfall, they were in plain view and in perfect condition, resting on a clump of broom grass directly in his path. They looked, Dave realized, as if they had been waiting to be found.

"I have always believed in miracles, but so often they seem to happen to someone else," Dave says. And maybe that's because *we* so often forget to ask. "The glasses reminded me that he wants to be involved in every part of our lives. No problem is too small for God."

WITH LOVE, FROM ABOVE

Who can say that the time will not come when, even to those who live here upon earth, the unseen world shall no longer be unseen?

—Phillips Brooks, Episcopal bishop

"One afternoon shortly after my friend Beth died, I was weeping at her loss," says a Wisconsin woman. "Suddenly my house was flooded with the scent of her favorite perfume. I smell it now, at occasional moments. I believe Beth is sending me a sign that she is with God."

"As our mother died, the entire room was lit in a beautiful golden glow," another woman wrote. "For a moment we seemed to glimpse eternity, and it brought us great comfort."

Stories abound of mourners being reassured by those who have gone on to heaven. A caress, a vision, or just a little signal. Perhaps they are God's way of letting us know that our loved ones are safe in his arms.

A woman named Carol approached the table, where I was signing books, with an inspiring story. Her mother had had Alzheimer's disease, and had been very difficult to care for. One day Mom spotted a beautiful antique doll in a mail-order catalog. "I'm going to get that for you," she told Carol.

Carol sighed. She collected similar dolls, but this model was very expensive, and her mother had lost all awareness of price. Nor had Mom been able to buy anything for some time—shopping was too confusing for her. "Mom, I don't need any more dolls," she said gently.

"Yes!" her mother insisted. "You're going to have it. I promise!"

Carol knew that the doll represented her mother's frustrated attempt to express love for her daughter. Her inability to do this was painful for both of them.

During the next difficult weeks, her mother talked constantly about the doll, asking if she had ordered it, and why it hadn't arrived. "It's on the way," she told Carol again and again. A few weeks later, the elderly woman died.

Several months after her mother's death, Carol's son went to a garage sale and brought home a box filled with loose trinkets, including pieces of a doll. Intrigued, Carol put the doll together. It was the antique model in the catalog, right down to its tiny shoes and perfect dress. Her mother's last gift had, indeed, been "on the way."

Dan Paluscsak's father had purchased an old farmhouse in Medina, Ohio, for his family to live in, and it needed a lot of work. "Dad was very handy, and he enjoyed doing repairs and remodeling," Dan says. Mr. Paluscsak hammered and sawed almost every night, but always cleaned up the work area and replaced his tools neatly in his workshop. No one else ever touched them.

When Dan was twelve, his father died suddenly, following a series of strokes. His current project, remodeling the upstairs, came to a halt. "During Dad's funeral, our minister reminded everyone of how much Dad enjoyed his carpentry work," Dan recalls. "And he emphasized John 14:3: 'I go to prepare a place for you.'"

Young Dan missed his father very much during the following months. He wondered if perhaps God had "prepared a place" for Mr. Paluscsak that involved a remodeling job in heaven. Was his father happy, fulfilled? How would Dan ever know?

One morning when Dan was in the living room, he saw movement at the door to his father's workroom. "Incredible as it sounds, my dad walked out of his shop carrying his hammer, saw, and carpenter's square," Dan says. The figure then went up the stairs and disappeared from view.

Dan doubted his sanity, and decided to keep the vision to himself. Later, however, he and his brother went upstairs to play.

"Look, Dan!" his brother said, pointing to the front unfinished bedroom.

Dan stared. There on the floor lay his father's tools, the same three he had seen Dad carry upstairs.

Dan told his mother about his experience. They decided that God must have wanted them to know that Mr. Paluscsak was indeed safe, happy, and still doing what he enjoyed. "I kind of like to think that God is using Dad to help prepare *our* place in heaven," Dan says today.

Occasionally God permits our loved ones in eternity to become more personally involved in our lives.

Donna Victory was eighteen years old in 1983 when her mother, Janice, died. She found the void unbearable. "Our family had been very close, and Mom just lived for my dad, my two younger brothers, and me," Donna recalls. "She was my best friend. And maybe the saddest part was that she had always dreamed of being a grandmother. Now, if any of us became parents, she wouldn't be around to enjoy it."

The family grieved, but as time passed, Donna tried to adjust. Three years later, she married. The couple moved to Sherman, Texas, and soon Donna became pregnant.

"As the baby grew, I had five sonograms, and all indicated that we were going to have a girl," Donna says. But the last test also showed that the umbilical cord was wrapped around the baby's neck. Donna's physician put her on bed rest for the remainder of her pregnancy. "They told me that labor and delivery would be all the stress our little daughter could handle," Donna says, "so I sat around, did nothing—and worried." Away from her family in Oklahoma, Donna thought frequently of her mom. How she longed for the reassurance that only a mother could provide!

When labor began, it seemed to progress normally. But everyone was watchful as the birth became imminent. Would the infant be all right? Suddenly Donna froze. "They were telling me to push—but I was so afraid—I thought she would be born dead, and I didn't want it to happen."

Then, inexplicably, her terror receded, and she felt flooded with peace. A woman was speaking to her: "Don't worry, Donna, everything's okay. He's fine." Was it a nurse? No, it was her mother— Donna was sure of it—and Janice had called the baby *he*, not *she*. Strength filled Donna, and she pushed with all her might.

"It's a boy!" her doctor said, moments later. "What a surprise!" But not to Donna. Janice had already brought the joyful news.

As Donna cared for little Brent, she began to feel less alone— after all, hadn't her mother been with her in the hospital? Surely Janice was still near. "I told the baby all about Mom, to keep her memory alive for him," she says. Later, when baby Dustin arrived, he, too, heard about the wonderful grandmother who had wanted so much to meet them here on earth, but who, instead, was watching over them from heaven, along with all the angels. "I guess I considered her the boys' special guardian," Donna says, "even though I wasn't sure—at that point—that I actually believed in angels."

One summer, when the boys were almost three and four, they "graduated" to bunk beds. To save space in their room, Donna stacked the beds. She assumed that Brent was old enough to sleep on the top bunk and would enjoy the adventure. But Brent was afraid of heights and balked. Toddler Dustin, on the other hand, couldn't be kept *off* the bunk, climbing up whenever Donna's back was turned. "I didn't want Dustin to sleep on top," she says. "I thought he was too young and too small. But we tied a two-by-four board up there for a guardrail, so I finally agreed."

Dustin had been sleeping on the top bunk for a few weeks when one night Donna abruptly awakened. Confused, she sat for a moment in the dark bedroom. What was wrong? Nothing seemed out of the ordinary. Her husband, a night security guard, was at work, and everything was quiet. But she felt a sense of urgency, as if someone had deliberately shaken her awake.

Donna looked over at the doorway. Her mother was standing there.

"She looked like she always did, except she was in a kind of mist," Donna says. "She seemed to float, as if she was walking on air." It was impossible! Surely Donna was hallucinating—yet she felt no fear or bewilderment.

Her mother did not speak. Instead, she motioned for Donna to follow her, and Donna did, without question. The two went down the hall to the boys' room, then Janice stepped aside so Donna could enter.

Brent was lying on the bottom bunk, asleep. But Dustin . . . Donna gasped, horrified. The toddler had somehow slipped between the mattress and the piece of wood, and had gotten caught. He was hanging limply in the air, his feet dangling above the bottom bunk, his neck held fast by the guardrail!

Oh, God! Her hands shaking, Donna freed him. Was he still breathing? Yes. In fact, he seemed to be sleeping soundly, normally. Trembling, Donna burst into tears, holding Dustin close to her. How much longer could he have hung there before his airway had been completely blocked, and he had quietly died? And she would never have heard a thing!

In the midst of her weeping, she felt a gentle, reassuring hand on her shoulder. She turned, but there was no one there. She was alone. But not *really* alone at all.

"I haven't felt my mother's presence since, but my brother, who now has a baby, told me recently that he thought he saw Mom bending over the crib," Donna says. "It makes me feel even surer that she is in charge of all her grandchildren. And knowing that, I am at total peace."

PROMISE ON PAGE ONE

To reach the port of heaven, we must sail sometimes with the wind and sometimes against it, but we must sail, and not drift, nor lie at anchor.
—OLIVER WENDELL HOLMES

How did people here handle such terrible heat, Reneé Smith mused on the morning of August 1, 1983, as she put her two little daughters into the car for a shopping trip. The Smiths had moved to Lincolnton, Georgia, from Franklin, North Carolina, a month ago, but Reneé doubted she would ever get used to summers in the Peach State. Today was overcast, too, and gloomy, with water almost hanging in the air. Perspiration ran down her face as she buckled three-month-old Sarah into a little carrier seat in the front of the car, fastened five-year-old Jessica's seat belt, and pulled into traffic.

"Are we almost there, Mommy?" Jessica asked from the back of the car as they drove the twenty miles to Thomson.

"Almost, honey." Reneé passed a temperature sign. It was now 105 degrees.

Reneé pulled into the Kmart parking lot at 1:35 p.m., turned off the engine, stepped out of her car, and started to pick up Sarah in her carrier seat, as Jessica exited from the other side. It was the last thing either of them remembers. Witnesses were left to reconstruct the event—a sudden *pop*! and a bolt of lightning striking the Smith car, springing off on both sides. One flash hitting Reneé on the left temple, the other hitting Jessica in her left eye. Reneé dropping the baby and collapsing into a puddle on the pavement. Jessica falling on the other side of the car.

A woman in a nearby car got out and ran to Reneé. She began to pray over her. Although baby Sarah seemed alert and unharmed, Reneé's eyes were rolled back in her head. There were no signs of life. An off-duty medical technician dashed up. She confirmed that Renee's condition was grim. "No pulse, no breathing," the technician told the woman after a quick exam. "I'll start CPR—you keep praying." It began to rain, and the frantic Kmart store manager who had just arrived at the scene raced back inside to get blankets.

A man parked in a pickup truck had seen the whole thing. He reached Jessica and began breathing for her. The little girl had no heartbeat either. Her shoes had been knocked off by the lightning and were on the other side of the parking lot.

After about ten minutes, Jessica revived. "Where's Mommy?" she asked the worried man bending over her.

"Your mommy's going to be fine, honey," he reassured her. But he knew as well as anyone in the rapidly forming crowd that Reneé had been electrocuted, and had almost certainly died.

The ambulance arrived, and all three victims were loaded onto stretchers. Personnel worked frantically on Reneé as the vehicle sped toward McDuffie County Hospital in downtown Thomson. No pulse, no heartbeat. "Defib! Defib again—stand clear!" On the third try, some seventeen minutes after Reneé had been struck, workers were able to restart her heart in an erratic beat, while a machine breathed for her. The ambulance crew looked at each other in despair. This woman was so young, and yet there was little hope that she would survive.

Physicians at McDuffie agreed with the ambulance workers. An inch-wide burn mark went from the top of Reneé's head down to her spine, melting her hair to her head. Bruises clearly marked her left temple, where the lightning had entered, and her left hand, where it had exited. Her eyes rolled around as if disconnected, with no focus. Since University Hospital in Augusta had a critical care unit, physicians decided to send all three patients there. But in their opinion, Reneé had suffered irreversible brain damage and was in a "nonrecoverable" state.

While this was happening, people were trying to find Reneé's husband, Fred, a telephone installer. When his supervisor finally located him, he told Fred only that Reneé and the girls had been in a serious accident. Panic-stricken, Fred raced home to change his clothes, wet and muddy from the rain. He didn't even know where University Hospital was, he realized as he sped along—precious time was going to be wasted as he searched for directions. And how could he face what might have to be faced there alone? "God," he prayed, "send someone to come and be with me, please."

Skidding to a stop in front of his house, Fred saw a man standing there—his new pastor, Mike McBride, from First Assembly of God in Lincolnton. "Someone just called and asked me to meet you," the pastor explained. "We thought you would want someone with you."

"I do. Thank you." Fred was slightly relieved, but his anxiety continued. Reneé, his daughters . . . Love for them overwhelmed him.

As the two men sped toward the hospital, Fred's panic suddenly receded. In its place he felt a profound sense of peace. Words came to him, from 2 Timothy 1:7: "For God did not give us a spirit of cowardice but rather of power and love and self-control." Fred would *fight* for his family with his love, standing on the promises of God. He looked over at Mike McBride. "I have a God who heals," he said with determination. "He's going to heal my whole family."

The pastor hoped so, and the two men prayed together as the miles sped past. But as they entered the emergency room, a nurse drew Mike aside. "I think you'd better prepare Mr. Smith," she murmured. "No one expects his wife to survive the ride from McDuffie. She's going to be dead on arrival."

Fred remained steadfast, however, even when Renee arrived and he was finally allowed into intensive care to see her. She had not yet died, but she was in an unresponsive state, on a respirator, and jerked constantly due to muscle spasms. She certainly didn't *look* healed. "If she survives," one physician explained gently to Fred, "she could have nerve damage, kidney damage, paralysis, muscle damage, seizures, memory loss."

But Fred had made a decision to walk by faith, not by sight. And that marvelous sense of peace and love was still with him. As he left the hospital room, he ran into an Augusta Chronicle reporter roaming the halls, sent to write a story about what had happened. "God is going to heal my whole family," Fred told the reporter. "Put it on the front page."

"But?" The reporter was at a loss. Wasn't this man's wife almost dead?

"Put it on the front page," Fred repeated.

The reporter did. Another writer, from the Augusta Herald, picked up the same story. The entire community waited.

A few days later, both little girls were sent home in good health. It was determined that the rubber in the infant carrier had acted as a shield, keeping baby Sarah from sustaining any injuries. And although Jessica had developed red streaks running up and down her body—possibly blood clots forming as a reaction to the heat—they had mysteriously disappeared moments later, after Fred had gone out in the hospital hallway and simply said, "God, you've got to do something."

Reneé remained in a coma. People all over Augusta prayed for her well-being, and prayer groups filled the hospital waiting room. At one point, while outside Reneé's room, a man broke into tears. "Did you see them?" he asked those around him. "Three huge angels wearing gold and bronze. They went through the wall into her room. They're doing battle for her life." No one else had seen his vision. But it was not hard to believe.

Three days after being struck by lightning, Reneé Smith awakened. "What did I have," she asked Fred groggily, "a boy or a girl?"

"You didn't have a baby, honey," Fred answered, tears welling. "You were struck by lightning."

"I can't see very well," Reneé murmured. "Everything is so blurry."

That didn't matter. Reneé was talking, aware. Fred had already received his miracle. If the lightning had damaged her eyes, they would find the strength to deal with that.

Then Reneé remembered something—she had been wearing contact lenses when she was struck. Perhaps one of the doctors had removed them when she was unconscious.

The doctors were horrified to hear this. Reneé *couldn't* have been wearing the lenses, they explained. For if she had, they would have melted and blinded her.

But she had been. The lenses were never found, and there was no damage at all to her eyes. And no permanent damage to the rest of her either.

"Aside from my feet being numb for a while and a reaction to some medication, I had no side effects," Reneé reports. Dubbed Augusta's "Lightning Lady" by the Chronicle, she was amazed and grateful at the blessings that flowed from what appeared to be a tragedy. For a while, she spoke about her experience in front of groups, and made many new friends. Money to pay the family's medical debts came from many (because Fred had just taken a new job, the family had no health insurance); and best of all, her miracle built the entire community's faith. "Our lives are truly orchestrated by an unseen hand," she says.

As for Fred, he's convinced that the faith he proclaimed so boldly had an influence on his family's restored health. "You never know what each day will bring," he explains. "But all things are possible if you believe."

SILENT PARTNER

What you are is God's gift to you.
What you make of yourself is your gift to God.
—ANONYMOUS

God never abandons us. But sometimes he permits valleys in our lives so we may more readily look *up*—at him. Perhaps this is why Lew Baker, a longtime alcoholic, went through two heart attacks and subsequent bypass surgery—along with diabetes—all during the same brief period in 1982. "At that time I knew of God, but I did not know him personally," Lew says. However, his health problems served as wake-up calls. While recovering, Lew began to read Scripture and listen to the experiences of those who had been spiritually renewed. Gradually his heart thawed.

"In March of 1983, I received Jesus into my heart and began to develop the close personal relationship that I now have with him," Lew says. At this moment of conversion, Lew also promised Jesus that he would spend the rest of his life helping others to kick drugs and alcohol.

A few years later, Lew, a long-distance truck driver based in upstate New York, was assigned to haul material for a road-building job in Maryland. To avoid heavy traffic, drivers often traveled at night. One evening at about eleven, Lew pulled out with a twenty-eight-ton load of concrete panels. It was a large cargo, but he wasn't apprehensive. His truck bore a GOD IS MY COPILOT bumper sticker, and with his faith growing deeper every day, what was there to fear?

"About halfway across Pennsylvania, the steering seemed to loosen up, and the whole front end of the truck acted like it was floating on air," Lew says. He pulled onto the shoulder, placed some warning flares, and checked everything he could. Three other truckers also stopped to help, but they found nothing. Lew drove carefully to the next truck stop, but by now everything seemed to be fine. Mechanics there could find no problem, either.

Had it been his imagination? Lew reached the job site in southern Maryland safely, and once again had his truck checked. Nothing. Nor was there any difficulty on his way back to New York. "When I arrived there, I reported the happenings to my supervisor," Lew says. "He assigned me a different truck until mine could be thoroughly checked out." Four days and three mechanics later, Lew's truck was returned to him. No one had found anything to fix.

"For the next few months I continued to drive back and forth from New York to Maryland with an occasional flutter or strange light feeling in the steering," Lew says. "Deep down I knew something was wrong, but I got laughed at whenever I mentioned it." Instead, he kept his growing concern to himself, and prayed even more frequently than usual.

One day Lew was assigned a heavy load of concrete to bring to the Finger Lakes area of upstate New York. The trip was uneventful until he passed the tiny village of Watkins Glen. "The highway was cut out of solid rock on the side of a mountain," Lew says. "Traveling up this steep, narrow road, I had solid rock on my right. On my left were drop-offs of three hundred feet or more, into a lake so deep that in some places, the bottom has never been reached." The truck engine ran hot and the radiator boiled as his truck strained to reach the top. Again the front end of the truck seemed light. Whenever Lew hit bumps or a rough stretch of road, it felt as if it was lifting off the ground.

Finally Lew reached his destination, made the delivery, and drove back to the shop. He pulled around to the back to have his truck serviced for the next day.

"I opened the hood and climbed up on the frame to check the water and oil," he says. "As I climbed back down, I started to slip and my hand went down against the steering gearbox mounted inside the frame."

As Lew watched in disbelief, the whole box swung completely away from its mounting plate. All eight bolts were entirely sheared off, and from their rusted ends, Lew realized they had been disconnected for a long time. He had driven over 5500 miles with a gearbox hanging in the air instead of controlling the truck's steering. Why mechanics had not found it, why he had not lost control of the truck, especially during his mountain climb, was something he could not answer.

The next day Lew removed his GOD IS MY COPILOT bumper sticker. "I knew then that God is the *pilot*," he says. And he hasn't forgotten it.

Today Lew is a counselor in three state prisons and two county jails, bringing hope and spiritual faith to inmates there. He can tell them with complete assurance that no one travels through life alone.[5]

BENDING THE RULES

The world will never starve for want of wonders,
but only for want of wonder.

—G. K. CHESTERTON, *TREMENDOUS TRIFLES*

Lew Baker is not the only person to experience a suspension of the laws of physics. And since God made the universe, he can surely bend its rules whenever he chooses.

Eighteen-year-old Bill Clarke, of Staatsburg, New York, discovered this when he went to work for some family friends who install air-conditioning systems. Bill was a gofer—someone who ran around the site picking up items and bringing them to the installers. His mother, Martha, was pleased with Bill's emerging maturity. But, like many parents, she was having a little trouble letting go. "Every day I asked God to reassure me that I had done a good job getting Bill ready for the adult world," she says.

On one extremely hot day, Bill and his two bosses were installing air-conditioning in a large luxury home. They had already dragged

110-volt lines through the attic ducts, and now they were working outside, near the home's inground pool. "Bill!" the boss called. "Plug in that extension cord, and bring it to me."

Bill did as he was told. Then he walked backward toward his boss, unwinding the cord as he went. No one saw Bill backing up toward the swimming pool—until it was too late. Still holding the cord, Bill plunged into the water.

Someone totally submerged and holding a live electrical cord should be severely burned or shocked, if not electrocuted. Furthermore, Bill's boss had just checked the main switch, and it was working fine. But nothing happened to Bill. Still holding the cord, he swam to the side and climbed out, unharmed.

"Bill! What happened? Are you all right?" Astonished, the men inspected the cord and the outlet. Power was definitely flowing through them. No one could imagine how Bill had escaped serious injury.

But when Martha heard the story, she realized its spiritual significance. "I knew then that I could safely give my son into the Lord's care," she says. "I will always be grateful for this special example of his power and protection."

Jim called radio station WYLL in suburban Chicago about a friend, Norma, for whom he had been praying. Norma, a single parent, was estranged from God and living a reckless life. She worked as a cashier, but was perpetually stressed and in debt.

"One night things got to be too much for Norma," Jim related, "and while she was closing her register, she stole four hundred dollars and put it in her purse." Heart pounding, Norma got to her car without being caught. But when she turned her key in the ignition, nothing happened.

She had just had the car fixed! It couldn't be—not another debt! Norma felt as if her world were caving in. She looked around the parking lot for help. Usually there were several coworkers pulling out. But tonight, oddly, the area was completely deserted. She had no one to call on, no one except . . .

Norma put her forehead on the steering wheel. "God," she prayed silently, "I haven't been close to you, haven't given you a thought in a long time. But for some reason, I seem to feel your presence. Please guide me now."

She waited a moment, then slowly got out of the car. Walking back into the building, she found her boss. "Here," she said, handing him the four hundred dollars. "I made a mistake."

Her boss looked at the cash, then at her. "I see," he said slowly. "Well, I'm glad you discovered it."

They smiled at one another, and Norma felt her heart lift. She could have been fired, even arrested. But for some reason, her boss had faith in her.

Maybe she could have faith in herself, too. Maybe it wasn't too late to start living God's way instead of her own. Norma went back to her car and tried starting it one more time. The engine roared.

Martha Malham and her husband, Howie, were in Arizona visiting their son, daughter-in-law, and grandchildren. "I poured a mug of freshly made hot coffee and put it on the kitchen table for Howie," Martha recounts.

Engrossed in conversation, none of the adults saw eighteen-month-old John Paul toddle over, reach up, and grab the container by the handle. He tilted it, and the scalding coffee cascaded out of the mug toward his upturned face.

Everyone froze in horror; then suddenly the steaming liquid changed course, midair. "The coffee went flying at a forty-five-degree angle, completely missing John Paul's face," Martha says. "It landed with a huge splash on the kitchen floor and covered every-thing nearby. Yet not even a drop touched his clothes."

Who placed a protective yet invisible barrier around this little boy? Martha thinks she knows.

Fourteen-year-old Karen Costello's parents both worked, so she spent a lot of time alone with her stepbrother. Eric,* age fifteen, was always in trouble, and had even spent some time in jail. Karen was a little afraid of him.

One summer day as Karen sat on the floor watching television, Eric came into the house carrying a rifle. "Where did you get that?" Karen asked, shocked.

"I traded it off some kid," Eric answered nonchalantly. Then he lifted the rifle, aimed it at Karen, and pulled the trigger—again and again and again.

"Don't you know you're never supposed to point a gun at anyone?" Karen screamed, terrified.

Eric laughed. "Oh, don't be such a baby. It isn't loaded," he answered, looking at the rifle closely. "I'm going to trade it back tomorrow. This thing is a piece of junk."

Karen was relieved. Since Eric was planning to get rid of the gun, she decided not to mention the episode to her parents that evening.

The following morning Karen awoke and started to get up. Her normal routine was to get her robe out of the closet, then go to the kitchen for breakfast. But for some reason she decided to lie in bed just a few minutes longer.

Bam! A loud noise broke the silence. Karen saw a piece of wood rip from her closet door, exactly where her head would have been if she were inside. A hole suddenly appeared in the wall opposite the closet. The noise had been a bullet, whizzing through her room!

Eric raced through her bedroom door, his face the color of milk. "Are you all right?" he yelled. "Karen, I didn't know it was loaded! I swear it! I never put any bullets in it. I don't have any!"

Shocked, Karen stared at him. Obviously that bullet had been in the chamber the previous day when Eric had pointed the gun at her, yet he had repeatedly pulled the trigger. What had prevented the bullet from leaving the chamber then? What had prevented her from getting up just a few seconds earlier and being in its path now?

Despite her difficult family life, Karen felt less vulnerable after that. She knew God was watching out for her.

Falls (or potential falls) seem tailor-made for the suspension of physical law. While going through a difficult pregnancy, a young woman tripped at the top of a flight of stairs. In that first split second, she panicked, sure that she would fall and lose her unborn child. "Then everything went into slow motion," she reports. "I glided down the stairs. It was like falling through heaven." She landed as if on a pillow, and when their son was born three months later, "we named him Nathan, which means 'gift of God' in Hebrew."[6]

Barbara Gove was visiting her brother in Milton, New Hampshire, when her fourteen-year-old nephew, Eddie, jumped off a truck parked in the yard. Eddie started to scream in agony. Horrified,

Barbara saw that he had landed on a board with a nail in it, and the nail was now almost all the way through his foot. Eddie's dad was at work, and there was no one else at home. What should she do?

Barbara lifted her sobbing nephew into her arms, the board and nail still attached to his bleeding foot, carried him to her car, and drove him to the nearest hospital, praying all the way. Brakes screeching, she pulled into a parking space, picked Eddie up again, and hurried toward the emergency room entrance.

"As I carried him along the sidewalk, I heard a woman scream as we passed," Barbara says. "I didn't have time to stop and ask her why, so I just kept going." Eddie was awfully heavy, but Barbara finally managed to get him indoors and hand him over to a nurse. Then, as she stopped to catch her breath, she realized that the woman had followed her into the hospital.

"Were you screaming at me outside?" Barbara asked.

"Yes," said the woman, pale and shaken. "Maybe I'd better *show* you why instead of telling you."

The woman led Barbara back outside and showed her a large grate in the cement, almost the width of the sidewalk. It covered an opening where packages were dropped to the hospital basement. The grate was exactly where Barbara had walked. And it was open.

"I was sure you and the boy would fall right into that hole, and that's why I screamed," the woman said. "But both of you seemed to actually float right over it."

Barbara was astonished. How could this be? She knew her feet had never left solid ground. But later Eddie told her that he, too, had had a floating sensation as she carried him in her arms. And despite the doctors' concerns, his foot healed in just a few days, with no infection or aftereffects.

In 1987 Clem and Julie Walters went with their friends Sharon and David on a trip to Europe to celebrate the Walters' thirtieth wedding anniversary. Due to some research Julie was conducting, their major stop would be the childhood home and the convent of St. Thérèse, the famous Catholic saint from Lisieux, France.

Because they had been busy with pastoral activities in their prayer community during the days preceding the trip, "we were not well prepared," Clem recalls. "We didn't speak any foreign languages, and we were using Eurorail passes, which can be confusing. We were on a bare-bones budget, which didn't allow for mistakes. So we decided to pray our way along." Each morning the four would join hands, dedicate the day to God, and ask him for protection and guidance.

Things went more smoothly than they had expected. But on their way from Rome to Lisieux, problems began. Due to heavy rains, the train was delayed almost twenty hours, and when it finally reached Lisieux, the station was a madhouse. The four were on a tight time schedule due to various tickets that couldn't be exchanged, and now they had only a few hours left in Lisieux before boarding a ferry to cross the English Channel. "The women set out to find a map so we could locate the sites without delay," Clem recalls. "David and I stayed at the station to make ferry reservations by phone."

Since the men were unfamiliar with French coins, they couldn't operate the pay phone. They asked several people for help, but received only grunts or headshakes. Time was passing, and the convent was sure to be closing soon. Then an attractive, well-dressed young woman went to the phone next to them and, in rapid French, had a quick conversation. "Do you speak English?" Clem asked her as she hung up.

She turned to him with a radiant smile. "Of course I do," she answered. "How can I help you?"

Clem was surprised. Her English was flawless. Quickly he explained their need for reservations. The kind young woman made the call for him.

"It is all taken care of," she said as she hung up.

"This is wonderful. Thank you so much!" the men began to say.

"No need." She smiled over her shoulder as she walked briskly out of the station. "Enjoy your holiday!"

The two men followed, relieved. Ahead they could see Julie and Sharon standing outside a small shop talking to an older woman.

This woman, though speaking no English, had been able to help Julie and Sharon buy the correct map; moreover, she knew the route to the convent and wanted to drive them there. The women had tried to explain that they could not go without their husbands, and perhaps she would not feel comfortable taking two men along. She had not understood, and was still trying to persuade them. "It would be wonderful to ride with her. It would save so much time," Julie said. She was becoming concerned about missing her research opportunity. "But we can't bring you men along without her permission!"

Clem didn't know what to do. Just then the young woman from the train station appeared at his side. Where had she come from? "May I help?" she asked.

"You are becoming a lifesaver," Clem told her, and quickly explained. The two Frenchwomen conferred. "She would be happy to drive all of you," the young woman finally translated.

"Oh, wonderful!" Julie exclaimed.

Clem grabbed his camera. "Before we go, let me get a photo of you four women," he said, and quickly snapped a shot. Then the young woman melted away into the crowd, and the older one guided them toward her car. The couples did reach St. Thérèse's childhood home shortly before it closed, and Julie was able to complete her project.

The rest of the trip was pleasant, and the four often commented on the fortuitous arrival of the young woman in the train station. Without her help, their stop in Lisieux would have been ruined.

When they returned to Indiana, Clem took his rolls of film to a developer. One night he sat down to peruse them. He had used a good camera, and all the photos came out well, except the few he had taken in Lisieux. Something had blurred and darkened them, and the scenes were barely visible. It must have been a bad roll of film. Clem threw them into his wastebasket.

Later he had second thoughts. Why should those shots be ruined when everything else on the same roll—before and after—came out fine? Curious, Clem dug through the negatives and found the spoiled ones. He could see the scenes quite clearly in the negatives. Here was the snap of Thérèse's convent, another of her childhood home. Clem held up the next negative, the one he'd taken of the four women standing in front of the little store in Lisieux. His skin prickled.

There was no mistaking the pose or the background, and the little group was perfectly centered. But there were only three women on the negative—Julie, Sharon, and the older woman who had given them a ride. Where the young woman had stood, there was no image at all.

"We were never able to get an actual photo developed from that negative. It just never 'took,'" Clem says. Perhaps angels have that effect on cameras. But Clem has no doubt they were surrounded by heavenly help on that special trip, and still are. No problem is too minor for God.

Vision of Hope

It is a dream, sweet child! a waking dream,
A blissful certainty, a vision bright,
Of that rare happiness, which even on earth
Heaven gives to those it loves.

—Henry Wadsworth Longfellow, "The Spanish Student"

Phyllis and Gus Cavallari of Cleveland, Ohio, were married in 1965. Two years later, they delightedly discovered that they were expecting a baby. It would be the first grandchild, and both extended families were thrilled. Unfortunately, Phyllis soon miscarried. "The first thing I asked when I came out of the anesthesia was, 'Can I still have babies?'" Phyllis says. "I wanted to be a mother so much."

The doctors told her there was no reason not to hope. But the year dragged on, and nothing happened. Phyllis prayed, and tried not to become discouraged—she was still young, and time was certainly on her side. But she couldn't seem to shake her worry. Gus had been saddened by the miscarriage, but now he was even more concerned about Phyllis. He hated to see her so heavyhearted, and he was helpless to do anything about it. "Gus and I have always had a special love for one another," Phyllis says. A child would have made their lives complete.

The couple lived on the second floor of a two-flat house owned by Gus's mother. One beautiful summer afternoon in 1968, Gus went downstairs to visit Mrs. Cavallari. After he left, the apartment seemed very quiet, and Phyllis decided to take a nap. She felt tired—not really sick, but not her usual self, either. Maybe she was pregnant! No, somehow Phyllis knew her prayers had not yet been answered. The realization made her even more lethargic. She crawled into bed and pulled the sheet over her.

She had been sleeping for some time when she heard children laughing behind her. She decided they must be playing somewhere outside, and yet the sound was so loud, it seemed they were actually in the room. The giggling continued and irritated Phyllis. She rolled over—and stopped.

There, standing next to her bed and looking down at her, were two children, their faces wreathed in grins.

"The boy was about eight years old," Phyllis recalls. "He had black hair and black eyes, and was wearing a striped knit long-sleeved shirt. The girl was about four. She had long light-brown hair and big brown eyes."

Phyllis looked at the children in astonishment. Who were they? How in heaven's name had they entered the house and come up to the second floor without Gus or his mother hearing them? Should she be alarmed? But the youngsters seemed so relaxed, so delighted by the trick they had obviously played on her. They didn't say anything, but continued to giggle. "Be quiet!" Phyllis heard herself say, annoyed. "I'm trying to sleep!" And with that, she turned back and closed her eyes.

An hour or so later, Phyllis awakened to an empty room. Puzzled, she recalled the odd event. Why had she not thought to question the children about who they were, or how they had gotten into her bedroom? How strange that she had felt almost *comfortable* with them. Had she dreamt the whole thing? No—there had been nothing hazy or dreamlike about their presence, and her memory was as vivid as if they were still here. She could still remember their laughter, recall the boy's straight black bangs, the girl's happy smile.

All of a sudden, as if a lightning bolt had hit her, Phyllis knew who the children were. "They were mine, the children I would someday have," she says. She knew it as clearly as she had ever known anything. God had answered her prayer, and had sent her a vision to confirm it.

After that, Phyllis no longer worried about becoming a mother. In fact, much to Gus's relief, she became lighthearted, confident— and not at all surprised when she became pregnant several months later. "Those were the days before all the prenatal tests were available," she says. "I never had any tests, but I knew the baby would be healthy, and that it would be a boy." Serenely she purchased a sampler, and sewed "Louis" onto it, along with the figure of a black-haired, dark-eyed boy in blue pajamas. She waited only to add his birth date and his weight.

Louis was born November 17, 1969. He was a fine healthy baby, with straight black hair and black eyes. When Louis was a toddler, Phyllis had another miscarriage, but she refused to panic. God was sending her one more child, a girl, and he always kept his promises. She became pregnant again in 1973.

"This time I embroidered a sampler with the figure of a little girl, sitting on a pink rose," Phyllis says, "and sewed the name 'Christine.'" Her baby daughter was born September 6, 1973, almost four years after Louis. Phyllis added Christine's birth date and weight to the little-girl sampler. She never became pregnant again.

Louis and Christine grew to look exactly like the children Phyllis had seen. And they were also "gigglers," especially when Phyllis was trying to take a nap. "Many times I would roll over to see them standing near my bed and laughing down at me," she says, "and I would remember that wonderful day." From all eternity, the Father had known they would be hers, and for whatever mysterious reasons, had given her a glimpse of heaven.

RESCUE IN NASHVILLE

I am a link in a chain, a bond of connection between persons. God has not created me for nought. I shall do good, I shall do his work. I shall be an angel of peace, a preacher of truth in my own place while not intending it—if I do but keep his commandments.

—JOHN HENRY NEWMAN

Weatherwise, it had been a difficult May 1995 in Tennessee. Winds, flash flooding, and strong thunderstorms had already pummeled many parts of the state, and as May 18 dawned, weary residents braced for more of the same. By 8:30 a.m. in Memphis, gales had pushed a trampoline down the middle of a street and blown down several tents at an outdoor cooking contest. The city of Linden began closing roads because of flooding. In White Bluff, falling trees crushed a house; a Newcastle trailer tipped over. But in Hendersonville, a Nashville suburb, Jan Neve noticed only a drizzly rain as she left for her job as office manager at Haverty's Furniture

Store. "I called to my husband, 'I'll be home tonight!' as I left," Jan recalls. "But we never really know, do we?"

Around noon, a storm developed. From her office in the back of Haverty's, Jan watched it for a while through the large front display windows. The rain seemed odd, with a muddy sort of consistency, and she could hear the wind rising. Maybe she shouldn't go out for lunch. Two young coworkers passed her on their way to the break room. Suddenly the lights went out.

Startled, both young women screamed. "Don't worry. It's okay," Jan reassured them. She got up, went to her office door, and, with her right hand on the doorframe, leaned out. The break room had no windows, but she could still see into the darkened showroom, where customers were cautiously making their way to the front door. Rain pounded on the plate-glass storefront, and the sky looked dark and ominous. The lights came on again for a few seconds, flickered, and went off. Then, incredibly, the front of the store collapsed.

"It was shocking, unbelievable," Jan says. "No one knew what was happening. Had a jet plane crashed into our building? Was it an earthquake? We later learned that a tornado had touched down, and as the wind hit our building, which is on top of a hill, pieces of the front windows sailed through the air like Frisbees."

The deadly fragments bounced off walls, fell on screaming customers, and shattered into tiny pieces. The roof peeled away as five air-conditioning units crashed to the showroom below. Walls buckled, huge holes appeared in the ceiling. It was then that Jan felt the pain.

Dazed by the scene unfolding before her, Jan hadn't immediately realized that her right hand had been pinned to the wall as her office door and doorframe gave way. Now, although she could not see much in the semidarkness, her hand felt as though it was being fried in a hot skillet of grease. "Oh, God, help me!" Somehow she managed to open the door with her left hand and pull her right one free. Horrified, she looked at it.

"I knew I was in trouble," Jan says. "The tendons were exposed, muscles hanging out, fingers going in all directions. It had almost been severed. Blood was pouring from an artery, and I realized that if I did not get help immediately, I would probably bleed to death." But the world was still whirling around her, customers screaming, plaster and glass falling. Jan dived under her desk for shelter while she tried to think of what to do.

She would call 911 immediately. She dialed awkwardly with her left hand. But the telephone was dead. The wind was quieting now, and Jan grabbed her mangled right hand with her left and ran for the front door. "I stepped over crying people, fell over tables, broken furniture, and debris. My only coherent thought was to get to the parking lot, get into my car, and drive to the hospital," Jan recalls. But could she make it while losing all this blood?

As she stumbled through the front door, she gasped at the devastation in front of her. Uprooted trees, electric wires, and light poles lay on the ground, fire racing up and down their length. Buildings were half-gone, and the street was filled with overturned cars and debris. Nothing was moving in any direction.

But she *had* to get to the hospital! Frantic, Jan raced for the parking lot. A coworker followed her, realizing Jan was probably half-mad with shock. "Jan, stop!" he cried. "We can't get out of the lot! Look!"

He was right, Jan realized, as she came to a halt, breathless and terrified. Trees and live power lines lay on top of almost every car in the lot, blocking the nearest exit. Fires were starting, and gas tank explosions would soon follow. She was going to die here, Jan realized. Help couldn't get to her, and she couldn't get to it.

Desperate, she turned around—and saw Robert Morgan in his black pickup truck.

Robert Morgan had been at Haverty's Furniture Store the previous day, checking on a job. His company had built a nine-thousand-square-foot addition to the store, and where the two structures were joined, water had started to leak when it rained. Robert had assumed the problem was fixed yesterday, but this morning from his office in Cookville, he had talked to the Haverty building engineer. Although there was only a slight drizzle in Nashville at that time, the engineer had reported that four small leaks had just sprung.

It didn't sound like much of an emergency, Robert mused as he left his office. Right now the sun was shining, and he was scheduled for a job in Crossville, in the opposite direction. "But as I got into my truck, on an odd impulse, I turned west toward Nashville instead," he explains.

As Robert drove down Interstate 40, the sun faded and he felt wind rising behind him. Gusts became closer, stronger. Rain began. What a day this was turning out to be, Robert thought, regretting his decision. As he approached the hill where Haverty's stood, wind shook his truck. "Things started flying through the air, and cars pulled off the road, but for some reason I just kept driving," he recalls. At one point he looked with disbelief at the rain. It was pelting the terrain on either side of him, but there seemed to be no drops hitting his truck. Almost as if he were wrapped in a protective cocoon. But that was crazy.

Then, as he pulled into Haverty's parking lot, the tornado struck, exploding the world around him. And he saw Jan running out of the store, a trail of blood behind her.

Jan stumbled up to the truck. This stranger was her only hope now. "Sir, would you please take me to the hospital?" she asked. "I'm bleeding to death."

"Yes, ma'am," Robert answered calmly, although his heart was racing at the scene around him. "But I'm not from around here. You'll have to tell me the way."

"I will." Jan climbed into the truck, still clutching her wrist. Blood saturated the front of her blouse and streamed down both her arms. She was beginning to feel faint, and the pain was almost unbearable.

And how would they even make it out of the parking lot? Robert headed in one direction, but a downed tree forced him to stop. Backing up, he turned, but debris blocked his path.

Suddenly a huge flaming electric wire fell toward them. It was going to hit the truck! "Look out!" Jan screamed.

Astounded, Robert watched the line stop—until his truck passed underneath it. As he looked back in the rearview mirror, he saw the line resume its downward direction and hit the ground in a shower of sparks.

Then, mysteriously, the other exit seemed to open up. Robert sped through it and down the street.

Here again were downed trees, live power wires, an auto dealership with hundreds of damaged cars, dazed and weeping people surveying the wreckage. Nothing was moving—except their truck. Robert held his vehicle on the road with one hand, and attempted to take off his belt with the other. Jan was very pale, he noticed, and if she fainted, he would not know how to find the hospital. "Here!" He thrust his belt at her, shouting to keep her awake. "Wind it around your arm. Make a tourniquet. Pull it, pull it!"

She did what he said. He was kind, protective, although she knew he must be as traumatized by all of this as she. Maybe he was an angel, she mused dreamily, sent just when she most needed one. She had always loved angels.

"Are we almost there?" Robert demanded. He had to keep this woman alert!

"Oh no," Jan murmured. She was growing more light-headed with every mile. "There's still a long way to go."

Robert fumbled for his cellular phone and dialed 911. "Where are you?" the dispatcher asked.

"Where are we, ma'am?" Robert asked Jan.

"On Galatan Road," she murmured. She could see an ambulance coming toward them, the only moving vehicle in sight. But it passed quickly, its sirens shrieking.

"You're headed toward Hendersonville Hospital. Just keep going," the dispatcher reassured him.

Robert obeyed. "There was nothing on the road but us," he says. "I realized that the tornado was about five hundred yards in front of us, because telephone poles ahead kept parting and falling, like a giant invisible hand pushing everything over. Live wires sparked, and stuff was flying everywhere, but it all kept missing the truck." Robert turned on the radio and heard that the tornado was traveling at about forty-five miles an hour. "Naturally I didn't want to catch up to it," he says, "so I drove about thirty miles per hour, slower than I wanted to go, but probably safer for us."

The wind continued to howl, rocking the truck, and suddenly a huge piece of wallboard with hundreds of nails in it sailed across the road into their path. He was going to hit it! Seconds later, the left side of his truck went right over the nails. Robert gripped the steering wheel, waiting for the blowouts. But nothing happened.

Jan was almost unconscious now. How was he going to find the hospital without her? And yet Robert knew he was not the only one looking out for Jan. "It was," he says, "as if we had an unseen hand over us. Something much bigger was in charge." And yes! Up ahead loomed Hendersonville Hospital. He sped into the parking lot. They had made it.

A visiting hand surgeon was just finishing an operation at the hospital, so Jan was given blood and immediately whisked away. Robert hung around the emergency waiting room for a while, to see if there was anything else he could do. None of the hospital's regular phones were working (Robert later learned that the cellular tower was also down), so he asked if anyone would like to use his. "Could I check on my children?" one woman asked.

"Sure." Robert gave her his phone. But her call would not go through, and she handed it back.

On Robert's phone, the last call is automatically saved, and if the "Send" button is pushed, it redials the number. "For some reason, I pushed the 'Send' button, and her call went through," Robert recalls. "I handed the phone back to her so she could talk to her children."

Three different people attempted to use Robert's phone during the next half hour. None of the calls would go through. But each time Robert pushed "Send," all the numbers connected. *He* made calls, too—to his wife, to Cookville, the furniture store, even Atlanta. The phone worked only for him.

At another point a physician asked Robert where he had come from, and how long it had taken him to get Jan to the hospital. When Robert described the route and the distance, several hospital personnel told him he must be mistaken. "On a good day, moving at a brisk clip, that drive would take about a half hour," they all agreed. Robert knew he had driven slowly so that he would not catch up with the tornado. He also knew that he had picked Jan up at 12:30, just a few moments after the tornado had touched down. How, then, had Jan been admitted to the hospital at precisely 12:45? "Impossible," everyone agreed.

But there was no doubt at all that Robert was a hero. During that critical fifteen minutes, Jan's blood pressure had dropped dramatically, and she had lost at least two units of blood. It seems certain that without him, she would have quickly died.

Eventually someone returned Robert's belt, and he left to salvage what he could of his schedule. Only the next day did he drive his truck back to Cookville, and take it in to have the blood cleaned up. Safe in the shop and no longer needed, his two left tires finally collapsed—from those huge, clearly visible punctures that the nails had made many miles ago.

Remarkably, although at least twenty tornados were sighted in the state, and property damage was extensive, there were no storm-related fatalities in Nashville on May 18. And after extensive surgery, Jan Neve is recovering well and still in awe of what God did for her. "I think, *in this entire universe, me?*" she says. "But God had everything in place—the hand specialist right on the scene, the protection along the way, and most of all, Robert Morgan, who hadn't even planned to be in Nashville that day. Robert will always be an angel to me."

"People who know me will tell you I'm no angel." Robert smiles ruefully. "But the Lord did have his hand on us."

And in case there was any lingering doubt, God left them yet another signal the day after the tornado. Officials from Haverty's home office had come to inspect the damage, and from just outside the store they followed a trail of Jan's blood to the exact spot where Robert had parked his truck.

They found a piece of metal lying on the ground that the wind had embedded in some plywood. The metal was formed in the shape of a cross.

ANGEL UNAWARE

Trailing clouds of glory do we come
From God, who is our home:
Heaven lies about us in our infancy!
—WILLIAM WORDSWORTH, "ODE: INTIMATIONS OF IMMORTALITY"

When a woman is fortunate enough to find the perfect hair-dresser, she doesn't want anything to change. That's why Marcia Wilson, a physical education teacher in San Gabriel, California, worried a bit as her pregnant hairdresser's delivery date approached. "I'll be needing a cut just after your baby is due," she told Randi. "Will someone be taking your place at the shop temporarily?"

"No, but I don't live far from you," Randi said. "I'd be happy to do your hair at my house."

At first Marcia wouldn't consider it. Randi already had a four-year-old daughter and soon would have a newborn. "Wouldn't I be imposing?" she asked.

But Randi assured her that it would be no trouble, and four days after Randi's new daughter, Nicole, was born, Marcia phoned to make sure Randi was feeling well enough to keep the appointment. "I'm fine," Randi said. "Come ahead!"

Marcia had never been to Randi's house, but she found it easily. As she got out of her car, she looked up at the house and noticed the long front windows and white curtains. There was a pretty little girl at the window, excitedly pulling back the curtains and waving at Marcia. "She's here!" Marcia heard her cry.

Randi's older daughter. The curtains closed, and Marcia smiled as she walked to the front door. Obviously the child could hardly wait to display her new baby sister.

When Randi answered the door and Marcia entered, however, there was no sign of the little girl. Baby Nicole was sleeping in an infant seat on the living room floor. Perhaps Randi had sent her older daughter to another room to play or watch television while she cut Marcia's hair.

The women talked, and from time to time, Marcia turned her head to look at the baby, dozing about fifteen feet from her. Eventually the little girl appeared again in the living room and knelt next to Nicole, her arm protectively encircling the infant seat. She said nothing, but looked at Marcia with obvious pride and delight, smiling widely.

Yes, the baby is beautiful, Marcia sent a thought to the child. "Your daughter is really pleased with Nicole," she remarked to Randi.

"She's enjoying being a big sister," Randi agreed. When Marcia looked back at the baby a minute later, however, the little girl had gone.

Randi went on with the haircut, and after a while Marcia realized that there wasn't a sound coming from the other room. "Your daughter is being very good," she said.

"Yes." Randi nodded. "She's been sleeping a lot since her birth."

"No, I mean your other daughter. It's unusual for a four-year-old to be this quiet for so long."

Randi's comb stopped in midair. "What are you talking about?"

"Your *older* daughter, the one in the other room." *What was wrong with Randi?* Marcia wondered.

Randi looked perplexed. "Mrs. Wilson, my older daughter isn't home today. She's with her sitter."

"But, who's the child who's been near the baby?"

"What child? There's no one here except you, Nicole, and me."

Stunned, Marcia looked at Randi. She *had* to have seen the little girl. She had looked right at her! And wasn't this child literally bursting with joy over the new baby, celebrating with such a proprietary air that one would think the infant belonged to *her*?

It was then Marcia realized that something very special had happened. "I think," she said slowly to Randi, "that I have just seen your baby's guardian angel."

Today Marcia still can feel the glow of that wondrous day. "Angels don't only appear with harps and white lights," she says. They come, sometimes, when we least expect them.

PLENTY TO GO AROUND

A miracle is an event which creates faith. That is the purpose and nature of miracles.

—George Bernard Shaw, *Saint Joan*

An intriguing type of miracle is the multiplication of food or other items. Does God still do this? Or were these signs and wonders limited to early times? Ask Wendy Thaxter.

Caught in a bad Connecticut economy in 1991, twenty-two-year-old Wendy and her friend Sally drove to Iowa, where jobs were more plentiful. "We stayed with friends, then rented an apartment," Wendy says. Part of the apartment's appeal was the two young men who lived across the hall. The girls soon began dating them.

Sally and her boyfriend broke up, and she abruptly moved back to Connecticut, leaving Wendy with the last month's rent and other unpaid bills. Because she had no money for a security deposit on another apartment, Wendy accepted the men's offer to move in with them temporarily.

"Things were great for a while, but my boyfriend, Jack, soon started to change," Wendy says. "He grew moody and had a quick temper. Once he told me something that chilled me to the bone." Jack had said that when his wife had asked him for a divorce, he had considered killing her. He hadn't, because he didn't want their daughter growing up without parents.

Wendy was horrified. Then a friend warned her that Jack had started acting weird, and saying odd and hostile things about her. She would have to get away from Jack. But how? She still hadn't saved any money. When her grandfather in Connecticut became ill, Wendy decided to go home.

"I started shipping boxes to my mother," Wendy recalls. "Jack thought I was putting extra junk into storage." He *was* behaving strangely, and she was apprehensive about leaving. What would he do when he discovered she had gone?

One Friday night both men were out, and Wendy hurriedly loaded her 1986 Thunderbird and headed for a nearby motel. "I called my boss, explained my situation, and quit my job. She was very understanding," Wendy says. "Then I called my folks in Plainville and told them to expect me sometime Sunday evening." Wendy didn't tell her parents that she was in danger—why worry them? But she tossed and turned all night. Jack worked just down the street from the motel. What if he saw her car on his way home?

Saturday at 7:00 a.m., Wendy was on her way. She stopped to fill up on gas, then counted her remaining cash before getting on the expressway. Fifty-six dollars. No credit cards. Could she make it home on that? She would have to.

She stopped only once, in Indiana, where she ate and got gas again. By 7:00 p.m. she was somewhere near Toledo. She found a seedy motel room for thirty dollars, put another ten dollars into the gas tank, and phoned her parents. Now for a good night's sleep! But there were loud parties going on, and Wendy's door was thin with only a push-button lock. Sleep eluded her, but at least she had escaped from Jack. Just one more day and she'd be home.

She was on the road Sunday morning before dawn. "When I reached Pennsylvania, I started looking for the exit that would lead to Hartford and then Plainville," she says. "At some point I stopped and put my last five dollars into the gas tank." Wendy wasn't too worried, since she had only a few more driving hours ahead. Even if she ran out of gas a few miles from home, her father could come and get her.

But she had missed the turnoff, and when she saw the WELCOME TO NEW JERSEY sign, she knew she was in trouble. She wasn't supposed to be in *New Jersey*. It was close to six o'clock now, with bumper-to-bumper traffic in four lanes, moving at seventy miles per hour. She couldn't have turned off even if she had wanted to—or knew where to go. Near Paterson, she glanced at her gas gauge. It was resting on "E."

Wendy panicked. The tension of the previous days had finally caught up with her, and tears streamed down her face. The four lanes merged into two because of construction, then back to four again. Somewhere along the way, I-80 became I-95. Wendy kept driving, waiting for her car to sputter and stop. It was a nightmare.

Sobbing, she reached the George Washington Bridge and saw the $4.00 TOLL sign. It might as well have been four hundred. "Oh, God, what am I going to do?" she wept. "Please get me to Connecticut." She reached for her change purse—perhaps she had overlooked a few coins. Yes! Wendy counted out *exactly* four dollars in change, not a penny more. Now she could cross the bridge, pull over, find a phone.

"But now I was in the Bronx, and it wasn't safe to stop," she says. "I kept driving and crying and praying one long continuous prayer, 'Oh Lord, *please* get me to Connecticut, *please*, so I can call my parents.'" The gauge remained on "E," but the car kept going.

When Wendy saw the next automatic tollbooth, however, she almost screamed. What would she do now? Hysterical, she snapped open her change purse and looked inside, even though she knew it was empty. But it *wasn't* empty. Again there were coins there, this time a dollar's worth, the exact amount of the toll.

"I didn't fully realize how unbelievable this was, how my gauge stayed at "E" and my change purse kept yielding money," she says. "I just drove on, because there wasn't any way to stop. The roads were horrendous, and I expected to blow a tire any minute. If I slowed down, drivers would honk and glare. My nerves were as taut as they could get."

Then she saw it up ahead. A sign that read WELCOME TO CONNECTICUT. Again she wept, this time thanking God for answering her prayer. "I had just asked him to get me to Connecticut, so I expected to run out of gas as soon as I crossed the border," she says. "But I should have known God better than that. He wouldn't lead me all that way and then abandon me when I still needed him."

No, Wendy drove several more miles to Darien, where she found the first rest stop she'd seen since Pennsylvania. She placed a collect call to her worried parents, then sat by the side of the road until they found her, filled her gas tank, and took her into the restaurant to eat her first meal since breakfast. It was almost midnight.

"I believe I went at least four hundred miles out of my way that Sunday," Wendy says. "My car was packed and heavy, and it burns a lot of gas. It also burns the second half tank much faster than the first, especially at seventy miles per hour." So there was no reason that Wendy should have been able to drive for five hours on five dollars' worth of gas. Or pay tolls from a change purse that was empty. But she did.

"This experience was the turning point in my relationship with God," she says. "I was raised Methodist and I went to church until I was confirmed. But I didn't feel close to God in church, or anywhere else. I didn't think he had much to do with us until we died." But now she feels his loving presence every day. And she believes in miracles.

So does Hannah Lords, of Stanwood, Washington. She's experienced enough to fill several volumes. But perhaps that is because Hannah herself has spent much of her life making miracles for others.

When the last of the Lordses' six children got married, Hannah and her husband, Bill, decided to follow a longtime dream: working with the poor. They gave away their furniture and household items, and opened a storefront coffeehouse, called the Refuge, in an abandoned laundry across the street from the welfare office in Everett. In the back of the building they closed in a space for two bedrooms and a bath for their use. "Our desire was to give 100 percent of ourselves for the Lord," Hannah explains. "Living on the premises allowed us to channel Bill's wages as a truck driver, along with any other funds that might materialize, directly to our work."

At the Refuge, Hannah and Bill welcomed the addicted, the victims and the victimizers, and the homeless. "We fed them and kept music going as a gentle background of praise and Scripture to balance the pain that came through the door each day," Hannah says. "I cooked, cleaned, paid bills, prayed with people, conducted Bible study groups." And she began to encounter wonders, one after another.

One night Hannah saw angels—great white creatures standing among the rooftop vents, keeping watch over the Lordses and their work. Often, when praying over an intoxicated person, Hannah saw him become sober within seconds. And on one special morning, she witnessed her own multiplication miracle.

A group of young people who helped the Lordses had just arrived for a morning prayer session. The Lordses' daughter Linda was there, too, along with a police officer and a young man he had just picked up on a drug charge. The officer often brought troubled young people to the Refuge in the hope that their lives might be changed. The praying began, "and soon we were all caught up in a state of reverence, as if we were suspended between heaven and earth," Hannah recalls.

It was a blessed interlude, but as noon approached, Hannah belatedly realized she had left Bill's lunch on "low" in their rusty oven all this time. It would be a dismal and dried-up meal—two small slices of meat loaf and a little scoop of mashed potatoes, all that was left from last night's dinner. And these young people were hungry, too. How would she feed them? She hated to admit to their guests that God provided for their needs only *some* of the time.

Still praising and singing, Hannah slipped out to the kitchen. Linda followed, and laughed as she watched her mother impulsively plop twelve paper plates in a row. "Linda, I've never served one person without serving everyone," Hannah said. "I'm just going to put a drop of food on each plate, and that will have to be it."

From the oven, Hannah took the small pan of dried-up meat loaf and dipped into it with a large serving spoon. The spoon sank to the bottom of the pan, and when she pulled it up, it held two large, juicy slices of meat loaf! But the two original dried-up slices were still in the pan! Astonished, Hannah moved to the next plate, and dipped her spoon again. The same thing happened. Two more slices of juicy meat loaf materialized on the spoon. And again, and again!

"By now, Linda and I were laughing and crying at the same time," she says. "Could this be true, or were we just imagining things?" Hannah moved down the line of plates, repeating her actions. And when all twelve plates had lovely, moist meat on them—and the two original morsels still remained in the pan—she pulled the second container from the oven. In it were the dry, yellowed potato remnants. But when she broke through the stiffened crust, her spoon disappeared into fluffy, moist potatoes!

"At first I dropped a small portion on each plate, assuming I'd had such good luck with the meat that I'd better not push things too far!" Hannah laughs. But when all twelve plates held servings, more potatoes remained in the pan. She went around again, until each plate held a large white mound.

Then Hannah remembered a frozen head of lettuce in her ancient refrigerator. "Pulling the plastic wrap back, I felt it crackling in my hand," she says. "I hesitated, but the bit of green would make the plates more attractive." So she went down the line, breaking off chunks of frozen lettuce—only to have it turn into fresh, crisp leaves on the plates.

No one could have been more amazed than those at the table when Hannah told them what had happened. All rejoiced, and gave thanks to the One who cared so much for them that he had even provided celestial leftovers for lunch. "Linda and I had hated to leave the praise going on in the outer room," Hannah says. "But in serving others, we had been given an experience that would cause us to praise him even more!"

Pam Smith of Merkel, Texas, is no stranger to faith. When she worked as a waitress at a Pennsylvania truck stop, she often met hungry people and never turned one away. "I paid for their meals from my tips," she says, "and I was always richly blessed with an appreciative smile, a warm handshake, or a hug. And on those nights it seemed my tips were particularly good! I always had the funds I needed to live on, and I wanted for nothing." God, as Pam knew, cannot be outdone in generosity.

Last year, however, Pam and her husband ran into some financial difficulties. Money was very tight, and to make matters worse, Pam's elderly dachshund, Corky, developed severe health problems. "The doctor was very sympathetic, but he felt Corky would only live another week or so," Pam says. "I prayed a lot, and Corky started to recover!"

The vet considered *that* a miracle, but in order to stay well, Corky would have to take three different medications. Each was expensive.

"I am beginning to realize that I can go to my heavenly Father with anything," Pam says. "So with the faith of a child I said, 'Lord, I don't have the money I need for Corky's medicine, and I don't think I have the strength to lose him right now. But I'm placing it in your hands.'"

What happened? "For the past two months we've given Corky his antibiotic," Pam says. "We only purchased a month's prescription, but the bottle never runs empty." The dog's vitamin supplement, just a thirty-day stock, has lasted more than three months. And Pam cannot remember the last time she bought prednisone pills for Corky, yet there's always one there when she reaches for the bottle. "I guess the Lord loves animals as much as he loves us," Pam says. "All I can do is lift my heart to him, and thank him for our blessings."

While multiplication miracles once seemed rare, Bruce Simpson of Orlando, Florida, says he is hearing of more and more such instances. A very special one happened to him a few years ago, when he and his wife, Linda, were conducting a parish mission in Rochester, Michigan, a suburb of Detroit. Bruce, the father of six and an ordained deacon of the Catholic Church, also founded an outreach ministry, Good Shepherd Community, to sponsor days of renewal, prayer group teachings, retreats, and other evangelization work. The community is supported by donations, and a collection is usually taken for the Simpsons during a prayer meeting.

During that evening in Rochester, Bruce was asked by the leader, Bob*, to pray for his job situation. "Bob had been unemployed for quite some time, and he was at that age when it is often difficult, if not impossible, for a person to reenter the job market," Bruce explains.

While Bruce was praying over Bob, he suddenly felt as if he was receiving a message, sometimes called a "prophetic word," from the Holy Spirit. He drew Linda aside, told her about it, and asked her to pray with him for discernment. Linda did, and she, too, believed this communication was genuine.

The message directed Bruce to take one hundred dollars from their collection money, put it in an envelope, seal it, and give it to

Bob and his wife, Sheila. "For us, it was a large sum to give away," Bruce says, "but I did what I believed the Lord was directing me to do." As Bruce called the couple forward and handed them the sealed envelope in front of everyone, he also stated the rest of the words he had heard: "'This is a sign gift to you, a down payment,' says the Lord. 'I will provide, and I am going to open a door of opportunity to you, better than anything you have experienced before.'" Bob and Sheila were extremely grateful to the Simpsons, not only for the message of hope, but for the practical help. They left the meeting clutching the unopened envelope.

A year later, Bruce and Linda again ministered in suburban Detroit. Bob was there, and told them the rest of the story.

When Bob and Sheila returned home that evening with the envelope, they sensed that there was something sacred about it. "So we put it, still sealed, on the mantel," Bob related.

Several days later, the couple needed groceries, and they had no money. "Open the envelope and see if there is enough," Bob told Sheila. She did, and was able to buy their usual weekly amount.

A day or two later, they took more money out and put gas in the car. Then a utility bill came due, and they paid it from the envelope.

"After that, it was time for the mortgage and the other normal monthly bills," Bob went on. "We paid them all, everything, from the envelope. In fact, Bruce, that money kept us going for several months. It didn't run out until I was offered the best job I have ever had, a job that pays much more than my prior ones did." Bob looked at Bruce with tears in his eyes. "The Lord did open a door of opportunity for us, just as your prophetic word promised," he said. "But we never could have made it without your unbelievably generous financial help."

But it had only been one hundred dollars. Bruce's heart was pounding. What an honor to be part of such a miracle!

"I have sometimes joked with my family that I gave away the wrong envelope," Bruce says, smiling. But he knows what really happened. "Linda and I gave the little we had in obedience, like the boy with the five loaves and two fishes. And Jesus did the multiplying."

Stranger in the Fire

See, I am sending an angel before you to guard you on the way. . . .

—Exodus 23:20

Six-year-old Macy Krupicka and her family had just returned from Houston, where they had visited friends. The day had been filled with tornado warnings, typical of Oklahoma City in early July. Macy wasn't actually *scared* of storms, but when she went to bed that night she was glad that everything seemed calm. Her parents had already tucked three-year-old Amy and baby Kent into their beds. Then her father had locked the bolt on the back door in the den, as he did each night, with a special key. Macy knew that the door wouldn't open from the outside—or, for that matter, from the inside—without that key. "If I put the key near the back door, someone could break the window, reach in, and take it," Daddy had once explained to her. "So I keep the key hidden."

Daddy was always taking care of them, Macy thought now as she snuggled into her cool sheets. He was a little like God, she realized—at least, what she had just begun to learn about God. God and his son Jesus cared a lot about her, just like her parents did. Six months ago, Macy had walked down the aisle of the Village Baptist Church, and accepted Jesus as her Lord and Savior. It was a large commitment for such a little girl, but she had had no doubts. Now her eyes closed as she slipped into dreams.

It was midnight when a loud noise awakened her. Dazed, she sat up. Thunder. Yes, a big storm raged outside. Macy could see lightning flash. Was it the pounding rain that had roused her? No, she sensed it was something more.

She got out of bed and padded down the hallway toward her parents' room. There was something odd about the hallway. Smoke! Macy stopped, her heart pounding. Now she could smell the acrid odor and see something flickering in the living room. The noise had been lightning hitting her house, going through the electrical circuits, and setting the couch ablaze.

"Fire!" she heard her father yell. "Call the fire department!"

"The children!" That was Mom, sounding afraid.

"Mommy!" Macy cried. "Daddy!" No one answered. Did they know she was here in the hall? The smoke was thicker now, and tongues of fire stole across the living room ceiling toward the foyer where the front door was. Maybe she should try to get out that way—at least there was no bolt to unlock. But what if the flames jumped across the foyer and burned her? Frightened, Macy stood in an agony of indecision. She could hear her mother's frightened voice talking to the fire department on the phone. But she couldn't get to Mom.

All of a sudden, there was Daddy right beside her! He took her small hand in his, and she was flooded with peace despite her fearful surroundings. Instead of going toward the foyer, however, Daddy led her back down the hallway toward the other door, avoiding the flames. "Come this way," he said softly. "We're going out the back door."

In all this confusion, had he remembered about the key? But his grip was warm and reassuring, and she knew there was no need to fear. Daddy always knew what to do.

Macy did not see Daddy insert a key in the lock, nor did he let go of her hand. But the door opened easily, and then she was on the back porch, rain streaming down her face, soaking her pajamas. And Daddy was gone!

"Daddy!" she called. "Come back!" The back door was closed, but she opened it and peered into the den, now rapidly filling with smoke. "Daddy?" She went in and closed the door behind her, but it was dark. She went outside again, but everything was wet. "What am I supposed to do?" she asked herself. "Where *is* everybody?"

Bewildered, she entered the den again, closing the door behind her. Just then her mother came running in. "Macy, we have to get out!" Mom cried. "This door won't open. I don't know where the key is, so we'll go through the front."

"It opens, see?" Macy opened it. "I've already been outside. But it's raining."

"How?" Her mother stared at the door, then grabbed her daughter. "Never mind. Let's go!"

Macy and her mother ran through the wet grass around to the front of the house. They could see Amy and Kent by the front door on the porch. Little Kent's eyelashes and eyebrows were singed, and Amy was sobbing. Daddy was there, too, but he was trying to get back into the house, despite the flames. He hadn't seen them. They hurried toward him, but he disappeared in the smoke. "Wayne, come out!" Macy's mother screamed.

"Daddy went to look for Macy!" Amy cried.

"But I'm right here!" Macy shouted. Why was Daddy so confused?

Her father stumbled back onto the porch, a look of desperation on his face. "I can't find Macy!" he called to his wife. "The smoke is too thick in there to see anything!"

"Daddy! Daddy, I'm right here!" Macy shouted.

Her father stopped coughing. Macy watched as his frightened, hopeless expression turned to joy. "Macy!" he cried, running over to scoop her into his arms. "Thank God! Thank God you're safe! I tried to find you, but I couldn't cross the flames."

He peered into her face. "How did you do it, Macy?" he asked. "How did you get out through that locked back door, all by yourself?"

Although years have passed since the fire, Macy's mother, Juanita, still marvels at what happened, and what came later. "During the following months, Macy experienced no trauma or anxiety or nightmares, things that would have been normal in a young child," she recalls. "Instead, there was just a sense of safety and peace. How glorious God was, to care for her emotional well-being as well as her physical safety!"

And Macy? "I think I realized soon afterward that God had sent an angel to rescue me," she says. "But not just *any* angel. He sent one that resembled my father, because he knew that being with my father would make me feel safe."

Nor has she ever forgotten the touch of that hand. It sustains her now—as it did then—through fire and rain.

MARY'S MANTLE

All things bright and beautiful,
All creatures great and small,
All things wise and wonderful,
The Lord God made them all.

—CECIL FRANCES ALEXANDER, "ALL THINGS BRIGHT AND BEAUTIFUL"

When bombs fell out of the sky on Sunday morning, December 7, 1941, Pearl Harbor, Hawaii, was not the only city to suffer. Many areas in the Philippine Islands were also hit, including the city of Baguio. Baguio was a place of pine trees and mountains, surrounded by fields and gold mines, where Lolo Joaquin worked as an engineer. Lolo's family, all devout Catholics, had spent the weekend visiting him at the mining site, and everyone was driving home to Baguio for Mass when they heard the bombs exploding. Terrified, the family turned the car around and sped back to the relative safety of the camp. For the next several months, they and many others stayed near Itogon at a mission run by Father Alfonso, a Belgian priest and longtime friend.

Lolo had graduated from the Colorado School of Mining and had American friends, so as the Japanese army invaded city after city, he became involved in the resistance movement. He refused to work in the copper mines, knowing the metal would be turned into bullets used against his friends. His wife, Lola, smuggled messages inside loaves of freshly baked bread to American prisoners in concentration camps. But both knew it was just a matter of time before the Japanese made inroads into more distant areas, and discovered their activities.

Early in October 1942, as monsoon season began, word spread that Japanese soldiers were heading in their direction. "We'll go deeper into the mountains, to Dalupiri," Father Alfonso told the families that had been staying with him. They could hide among the Benguet tribe, whose kings were sympathetic to their plight.

The journey began early in the day, but Lolo soon realized that, for his family, passage was going to be difficult. Not only were the Joaquins traveling with four young children, but Lola had recently had a miscarriage and was still very weak. As miles passed and the trails became rockier, she often stumbled and fell. Other families tried to help, and Lolo knew that his was holding the rest of them back. With the Japanese on their heels, this could be disastrous for everyone.

"Go on ahead," he finally told Father Alfonso. "We'll catch up."

Father nodded reluctantly. "We'll send people back to help carry Lola as soon as we can," he promised. "God go with you."

"And you."

Soon their friends were gone. Frightened, everyone looked at one another. "Daddy, it's starting to rain." Nine-year-old Patricia glanced anxiously at the sky.

Lolo followed her gaze. Clouds were gathering, and the sun had dropped, leaving a chill in the air. "Come," he said, lifting baby Sonny into his piggyback sling. "Everything will be all right."

But it wasn't long before the wind picked up and rain pelted the little group. Soon everyone was soaked. The baby whimpered, and seven-year-old Teresita jumped as the trees swayed, whispering ominously. Lola grew increasingly exhausted. The monsoons had begun. How could they go on?

Soon the trail became so narrow that it could only accommodate one person at a time. To the right rose the cliff-side, straight up, stony and forbidding. To the left a precipitous chasm dropped to the overflowing river. The rain continued, pounding them as they struggled to stay upright on the slippery bluff. Finally Lolo stopped. "We'll sit now," he said calmly, although Patricia had seen the worry on his face before the last of the light faded. "Your mother needs to rest."

Slowly the family put down their packs and sat against the rocks. It was dark now, Lolo realized. Even worse, somewhere in the last mile or two, he had lost his way. What should he do? His little ones were exhausted—how could they continue across those treacherous cliffs, especially as night fell? But they couldn't sleep on the mountainside either, not with these heavy rains and soldiers trying to ambush them.

The wind grew wilder, and soon Lolo stood up again. "Perhaps we should crawl," he suggested. "One hand on the ground and the other on the wall of the mountain for guidance."

"Why don't we light a torch, Daddy?" Buddy asked.

"We can't, son," Lolo explained. "The enemy might see it and shoot us."

Teresita began to cry. "I'm scared, Daddy," she sobbed as thunder rolled across the mountains. "I want to go home!"

"Hush," he soothed her, patting her with one hand as he held the sobbing baby in the sling. "Stop crying, my little ones. This is not a good place to be caught by darkness and rain, but we must make the best of it. This situation calls for courage, not fear!"

"What can we do?" Lola asked, drawing four-year-old Buddy close to her.

Lolo paused. "We can pray," he said. "Haven't we always turned to heaven when things got bad?"

The children nodded. They had all read prayers from books, or recited those they had been taught. Of course they could pray. But now their father threw out his hands and lifted his voice in a way they had never heard before. "Cover us with thy mantle, oh Blessed Mother of God," he pleaded, "that we may be saved from all evil and temptation, and from all dangers of body and soul!"

It was a wonderful petition. It had power and hope, and their terror seemed to recede, just a little. Lolo felt it, too. "I have an idea," he said slowly. "It is too dark now to see ahead, but if we go in single file, each taking the hand of the person in front, we will all feel safer."

Teresita wanted to be brave. But she trembled as the river beneath them roared. "I'm afraid, Daddy."

Her father grasped her wet hand. "We will say the rosary as we walk, loud, so God can hear it over the storm! Buddy, you lead the way because you are the smallest and closest to the ground. Is everyone ready?"

"Ready." Slowly the little group moved forward, water streaming into their eyes, clothes plastered to their shivering bodies. They would not make it. One child would trip, and all would lose their balance, plunging to the canyon below. "Hail Mary, full of grace." Shakily they clung to the familiar biblical phrases, the reassuring cadence, the memory of their father's impassioned plea. They would not make it. And yet . . .

The journey seemed to last forever. But as they approached a sharp turn in the path, Buddy was the first to see. "Mama! Daddy!" he shouted. "Look!"

The rain had abruptly stopped, the air seemed sweetly fragrant. And before them, as far as they could see, stretched a long line of luminous candles winding around the curve of the mountain and on to a wide plain. But no—not candles. For these lights were bouncing, dancing, twinkling like stars illuminating the heavens.

They were fireflies! Thousands, *millions* of them, all hovering about three feet from the ground. In their combined greenish glow, Lolo could see the path as bright as day, even the footprints of the refugees who had gone ahead of them.

Awed, Lola dropped to her knees in thanksgiving. The children laughed, catching some of the little insects and wrapping them in their handkerchiefs. "We can use them for lanterns!" Patricia cried, delighted.

Clutching the baby, Lolo stared at the scene, incredulous. In all his life he had never seen such a huge collection of fireflies in the same place, or massed in a precise pattern like this. Fireflies didn't come during monsoon season. Nor did they hover close to the ground, preferring instead the tops of trees. Yet here, hip-high, were an incredible number, waiting for his family, enclosing them—like a mantle of protection, he realized suddenly. A queen's mantle, edged with gold.

There were more miles to go, but now the path seemed enchanted as the blessed fireflies lighted their way to the little village. Finally! They ran the last muddy yards and pounded on Father Alfonso's door.

"We had given you up for lost!" the astonished priest cried, coming out to embrace them. "How did you do it? How did you cross the mountains in the dark, in this raging storm?" Patricia and Teresita looked up. The deluge had started again.

"Father, we can't explain it," Lolo said. "Look behind us and see this miracle for yourself."

Father looked past Lolo. But there was nothing at all to see. No fireflies, no softened sky—nothing but darkness and streaming water. Lolo understood. "Has it been raining like this all evening, Father?" he asked quietly.

"It has not stopped at all, Mr. Joaquin," Father Alfonso answered.

The following day, Father Alfonso called a meeting of the tribal elders, some of them over one hundred years old, and showed them the fireflies left in Teresita's handkerchief. "Have any of you heard of this?" he asked. "Fireflies coming in a storm to light a traveler's path?"

The elders conferred. They were experts on the ways of nature, and fireflies. There was no possibility of such a thing, they all agreed.

Such a verdict did not matter to the Joaquins. For they had seen, not only with physical eyes but the eyes of faith. Life would be difficult as they struggled to survive in their war-torn land. But they would not be alone. How wonderful were the ways of God!

THE MAN IN THE PHOTOGRAPH

Most doctors do not regard these visions to be what they are—medicine for the soul, or maybe from the soul.

—MELVIN MORSE, *PARTING VISIONS*

It was especially cold that night as eighteen-year-old Johnny Bryan and his older cousin Donald left their home in Tulsa. The two were headed to the town of Vian, where Donald had lived until he'd moved in with Johnny's mom, Aunt Tressie. Donald's girlfriend still lived near the Blackgum Mountains, so each weekend he eagerly drove back to be with her. Because there were horses and open plains in Vian—and because he loved to ride—Johnny usually accompanied Donald.

That night Tressie Bryan tried to persuade the boys to stay home. "What if the car breaks down and you freeze to death on a lonely road?" she asked. But the boys laughed affectionately at her concern—didn't she know that weather warnings didn't apply to young adults? Tressie watched them leave and whispered a prayer for their safety. It wouldn't be much of a weekend for them if this snow and wind continued.

It did. Saturday seemed even colder, and by Sunday, Tressie was counting the hours until the boys' return. She was used to hard winters, of course. She was an outdoors person, part Cherokee, and her beloved brother, Buster, had taught her to hunt and ride at an early age. Those had been good days, the two of them racing across the fields, even sharecropping together, to help keep their younger siblings fed. And then they had grown up, the war had come—and everything had changed.

The last time she had seen Buster was during his final furlough before leaving for a place called Anzio. Buster had taken Tressie's husband aside. "Don't tell Tressie," he had said, "but I won't be coming home." When the telegram came, it had hurt so much that she had put all his photographs away. Her son Johnny had never even met him.

She was rambling now, using memories to pass the time, but she couldn't shake the feeling that something was wrong. As darkness fell, she paced restlessly, peering out at the snow-covered landscape. Where were they? Ten o'clock. Eleven o'clock. Midnight, and still no boys. They had never been this late before.

At 2:00 a.m. the phone rang. It was Donald, calling from the hospital in Broken Arrow, about twenty miles away. "The car skidded on an ice patch, turned over, and threw us out, Aunt Tressie," he said. "I'm okay, but Johnny hurt his leg. He's unconscious, so they're not sure if he has other injuries."

"I'll come right away," Tressie promised.

She prayed all the way to the hospital, and when she arrived, Johnny had regained consciousness. The doctors decided to release him. Relieved and grateful, Tressie and Donald helped him into the backseat of the car and adjusted his bandaged leg. Donald jumped in front, and Tressie drove carefully on the snow-covered highway. Johnny was a bit subdued, but seemed completely rational.

It was almost dawn when they reached home. Donald got out to open the front door while Tressie helped Johnny out of the backseat. He hobbled toward the porch with one arm around her shoulder. Suddenly he stopped. "Mom," he asked, "who is this man on the other side of me?"

"Why?" Tressie frowned. Had the bump on Johnny's head given him hallucinations? "There's no one on the other side of you, Johnny," she said carefully. "See? There's Donald, up on the porch."

Johnny said nothing more. The following day, however, Tressie broached the subject again. If her son had a concussion, she should report it to his doctor. "Johnny, why did you ask me about a man?"

"Mom, when I woke up in the hospital, there was a man standing at the door of my room," Johnny began earnestly. "One of his feet was crossed over the other as he leaned against the door, looking at me. He was wearing white pants, white shoes, and a long white coat, and his hair was jet black."

"I imagine it was the doctor," Tressie ventured. "You must have been confused from being bumped on the head."

"Maybe," Johnny admitted. "But when we drove home, that same man was sitting next to me in the backseat. He was looking at the buildings around us, like he was really interested. Then, when you helped me out of the car, he was at my side, until we got to the door. He looked at me and said, 'You'll be all right now.' That's why I wondered if he was someone from the hospital."

"No," Tressie answered. "There was no one in the backseat with you, Johnny." She was worried. Although the accident had turned out to be minor, Johnny was apparently more injured than she thought. What should she do?

She was still thinking about it later when the telephone rang. A nurse from Broken Arrow Hospital was calling. She and her husband had been driving behind the boys and were the first to come upon the accident scene. "It was the oddest thing, Mrs. Bryan," the nurse said. "When the car rolled over, its top hit the pavement in such a way that it formed a little dent. And that dent protected your son's head and shoulders before he was thrown out of the car." Johnny should have died from head injuries, the nurse believed. "But I wanted to let you know that I think he was being watched over, in a very special way."

Tressie agreed. Whatever Johnny's problems now, she was just grateful that he was alive.

However, nothing seemed to be wrong with her son. He never mentioned the man again, and resumed his life as if nothing had happened. Tressie remembered to thank God every night for averting a terrible tragedy and gradually forgot about Johnny's strange experience.

Years later, after Johnny moved out, Tressie was organizing a closet and came across some old family photographs. There was Buster in photos she had taken right before he left for Italy. "My favorite, one I had forgotten about, was of him standing with one foot crossed over the other, leaning against a rock," she says. "And there was another, a close-up of him without a hat." Tressie gazed at the photos. It was time to remember Buster again, she decided. She would have the pictures enlarged.

A short time later, Johnny popped in for a visit. He raided the refrigerator, then ambled into the living room, stopping in front of the photos now hanging on the wall. He stared. "Mom, I don't believe this."

"Don't believe what?"

"Remember years ago when Donald and I were in that accident?" Johnny's eyes were huge.

"Of course." Tressie would never forget that night.

"This is the man, Mom! The man I told you about, who was standing at the door looking at me! His foot was crossed, and he was leaning just like this."

"But that's impossible, Johnny. This is your uncle Buster. You've heard me talk about him. He was killed in the Second World War. You couldn't have met him, at a hospital or any place else."

"Mom, his face and that black hair are plain in this close-up. I've never forgotten him. He was with me in the car, and he helped me to our front door. And he said . . ." Johnny's voice softened in memory. "He said I'd be all right now."

Tressie thought of the accident and her son's astonishing escape, of the nurse's belief that he had been protected in a special way. Finally she thought of Buster, who had always cared for her. "I won't be coming back," he had told Tressie's husband. But who was to say that those who loved us on earth could not still love us from heaven?

"Johnny is grown now and has a family of his own," Tressie says today. "And I hope the man with the dark hair is still watching over all of us."

LOVE, FROM MOTHER

And yet, as angels in some brighter dreams
Call to the soul when man doth sleep,
So some strange thoughts transcend our wonted themes,
And into glory peep.

—HENRY VAUGHAN, "THEY ARE ALL GONE INTO THE WORLD OF LIGHT"

When Marvin Prince's father, William, died in 1972, Marvin decided to search out his remaining relatives. He knew William had several younger siblings in the Ukraine who had not emigrated to the United States when he had. "My father, the oldest, had planned to come here and make enough money to send for everyone," Marvin explains.

However, shortly after William arrived at Ellis Island, the First World War broke out. After it ended, the Russian Revolution began, and with the ensuing chaos, it was virtually impossible for William's family to leave the Ukraine. William's younger brother Michel watched their mother being clubbed to death by Russian soldiers in a pogrom. Another brother died later of mastoiditis. Then came the Second World War and the Holocaust. Michel's wife and two young children were killed by the Germans.

The devastation of his family had anguished William Prince to his last days. Now, Marvin decided, going to the Ukraine to reconnect with Uncle Michel was a gift he could give to his father.

Shortly after William's death, Marvin flew to Moscow, taking along his father's Bible, written in Hebrew and translated into Yiddish. It would serve as a bridge, he decided. "Since I spoke no Russian and my uncle spoke no English, Yiddish would have to be our common language, even though I remembered only a little of it from my childhood," Marvin says. Because Bibles were forbidden in Russia during the Communist reign, Marvin almost got arrested when he showed his at customs. But he was finally permitted to take it into Russia.

"When I put the Bible in my uncle's hands, his eyes filled with tears," Marvin says. "He had not seen one in almost fifty years. So I told him I would leave it with him permanently."

Michel declined, explaining that Marvin would be required to show it to the authorities on his way out of Russia. "But you will give it to me again one day," he promised.

"When, Uncle?" Marvin asked.

"In the world to come," the old man said.

Marvin was struck by Uncle Michel's obvious spirituality. He knew that, although his uncle's family had been orthodox and devout, Michel had completely turned against God after the slaughter of his loved ones. He had joined the Communist party for a time, and professed atheism. Who could have blamed him? But now he was again orthodox and prayerful. One night Marvin posed the obvious question. "Uncle Michel, why did you come back to God?" And the story, so long held in Michel's heart, came forth.

During World War II, the Russians had fought against the Germans. Michel was an officer in the Russian army and was captured. Because the Nazis were shooting Russian-Ukraine officers and Jews on sight, Michel stripped himself of his insignia and refused to speak. If he had answered his interrogators, they would have known he understood German—because it is similar to Yiddish—and he probably would have been executed. Instead, they assumed he was Russian and sent him to prison with the other soldiers.

Twice Michel managed to escape, and twice he was recaptured. On his third trip to prison—at the height of winter's bleakness—the Germans sent him farther west, to a maximum-security prisoner-of-war camp, surrounded by barbed wire, watchtowers with machine guns, and dogs. Michel's fellow prisoners constantly talked of breaking out, but Michel was depressed. The cold was horrifying, and this place seemed invincible.

One night as he slipped off into sleep, Michel had a dream. His mother was standing in front of him, young and healthy, just as he remembered her when he was a child. "Mama!" In the dream he stretched out his hand to her. But she did not smile.

"Michel, you must escape!" she told him.

"Escape?" he protested. "Mama, you've seen the dogs, the guns. I'd never find a way out."

"You must! If you stay here, my son, they are going to kill you!" His mother looked terribly upset.

"But how can I get out?" Michel asked her. "How?" Slowly she began to fade from view, and he awakened, heart pounding.

What a dream! It had been eerily vivid, amazing in its detail. He could remember her clothes, the familiar tender expression on her face. It was as if she had actually come to him.

But how odd. Not in his entire life, until now, had he dreamt of his mother.

Shivering from the cold, Michel turned over on the rough boards of his bed, faced the door of his barracks—and stopped. There, watching him, was a German soldier in full uniform. Was it a trick of moonlight? No, the man was real. But why was he here?

"Michel!" the soldier whispered. "Awaken your mates. You must all escape—now!"

Escape? Was Michel still dreaming? No, this was real. "I have nothing to give you," he told the stranger. If one could bribe a guard, one sometimes received better treatment. But to Michel's knowledge, no prisoner had been able to bargain an escape from this place.

"There is no need for bribes, but you must hurry." The German soldier pushed the barracks door wide.

It must be a trick. They would be shot as they ran to the fence. "We cannot get through that barbed wire, and you know it," Michel whispered.

"I will take care of that," the soldier assured him.

Michel stared at the door, remembering his dream and his mother's mysterious message. He had asked her *how*, and now she was sending him an answer. He shook his friends awake. They would take the risk.

The men darted outside, the German soldier in the lead. Now for the dash to the fence! Expecting a bullet in their backs at any minute, Michel and the others raced through the darkness. But although the moonlight outlined their shapes, and guards were certainly at their tower posts, no dogs barked, no guns fired.

Just a little farther. Now the fence loomed in front of them. Breathless, they stopped and stared in disbelief. A large hole had been cut in the barbed wire.

Michel looked around. The German soldier was nowhere in sight. If he had cut the wire beforehand, surely he would have been spotted by someone. How had this been done?

There was no time to think. Crawling through, the men ran alongside a river into the woods. Within moments they heard sirens, signaling a breakout. Dogs began to bark. "Quick!" one of the prisoners whispered. "Get in the water. It'll throw the dogs off our scent!"

"We'll freeze!" another objected.

Freezing might be better than being shot, Michel thought. And this whole night had been so strange. Along with the others, he jumped into the icy river and sat, in water up to his neck, until daybreak, when the search apparently went in another direction, and they made their way to freedom. None of the escapees ever suffered frostbite or other injuries resulting from their soaked, frozen clothing.

Although there were more hardships ahead, including another prison term, that night marked Michel's return to the faith of his youth. For surely his mother had journeyed across time and space to give him the encouragement he'd needed. And the German soldier? "He must have been a *malach*, an angel," Michel told his nephew. "What other explanation could there be?"

What other indeed, Marvin agreed. He, too, knew that heaven can touch even the most wretched place, and fill it with hope.

The God Squad

Even though you can't see us, we're always watching.

—Angels in the Outfield

A s a "street kid," Mike DiSanza learned early that life was full of dangers. He was small and slight, with a shaky self-esteem, and he soon developed a strong fear of any kind of physical violence. There was no use praying about his physical safety either; to Mike, God was an aloof deity, interested in rules and punishment, not concerned with an ordinary kid from the Bronx.

By the time Mike graduated from high school, the Vietnam War was under way. "There was no money for college," he explains, "and since many of my cousins and my brothers had been drafted into the army, I followed." Perhaps as a soldier he would overcome his fear of violence.

Mike came through Vietnam unscathed—but still anxious. Almost on a lark—and because few job opportunities loomed—he then took the test for the New York City police force along with fifty

167

thousand other applicants. Mike was astonished when he was one of the four hundred hired. Now he would *have* to get over his fears.

But he didn't. Mike worked as a patrol officer, first in Harlem, later in Manhattan. Due to antiwar sentiment, police officers were under attack by many, and morale was low. This increased Mike's on-the-job stress. "We were the cops on the front line, the ones who went into situations all alone," he points out. "I got seasoned real quick, but I continued to be afraid."

One evening on street patrol, Mike experienced such a deep anxiety attack that he thought he was dying. "My body literally shook as if it would explode," he says. *What was it all about?* he asked himself. *What was he doing out here in this high-risk environment, where fear tore him apart every night?* Just then a young black woman stopped in front of him and grabbed his hand. "Is anything the matter, Officer?" she asked.

Mike didn't answer, but he held on. "I didn't want to let go," he explains. "I felt something wonderful coming from her. I didn't know it then, but it was the love of Jesus, a love I had never experienced."

The woman led Mike to a storefront Pentecostal church, where people were singing, dancing, and praising the Lord. Mike thought it wasn't at all like the "flickering candles in those huge, formal New York cathedrals I'd been used to." A nameless hunger came over him, and a few nights later, he read the Bible at home for the first time.

He came upon the words of John 3:17: "For God did not send his Son into the world to condemn the world, but that the world might be saved through him." Mike closed the book. "Jesus, whoever you are, help me," he prayed.

A few weeks later, Mike answered a call for assistance from a fellow officer making an arrest in the subway at Seventy-second and Broadway. Mike ran past one officer still in the parked squad car and continued down the stairs. "The cop was attempting to handcuff the suspect, but he was resisting," Mike says. "A crowd was growing, and people were trying to rescue the suspect. I worked my way through and helped the cop get him cuffed. But we were surrounded. How were we going to get upstairs?"

The crowd was furious at the arrest. Hands shoved Mike toward the edge of the platform. "Throw him onto the tracks!" someone yelled. Mike felt a blow against the side of his head and heard, with dread, the sound of an approaching train.

"Jesus," he murmured. "Help."

Suddenly two large African American men loomed in front of him. "Follow us, Officer," one said. The other, somehow, made a little opening in the densely packed crowd. Relieved, Mike pushed the prisoner directly behind these two unexpected guardians. The crowd moved back, and with the other officer behind him, Mike and his prisoner followed the two men across the platform and up the stairs.

On the street, however, there was more danger. "Another gang had formed around the patrol car, and the driver was getting nervous," Mike says. "The black guys had been right ahead of us, running interference all the way." But now as Mike shoved the prisoner in the car and turned to thank his rescuers, they were nowhere in sight. How could he have missed them?

As the squad car pulled away, everyone sighed in relief. "Thanks, Mike," the subway officer said. "You did a great job getting us through that crowd."

"Yeah, thanks to those two big black guys," Mike answered.

"What guys?"

"The ones that said 'follow us.' You saw them. They muscled everyone aside."

The officer looked puzzled. "I didn't see anyone but you."

Mike stopped. He was getting a strange feeling. Just last night, in his ongoing quest to understand the Bible, he had read from Hebrews about "ministering spirits, sent from heaven to help in times of distress." Could the black men have been angels?

No. Police officers didn't see angels. Not unless they were having mental breakdowns. But although Mike's heart had raced during the subway episode, he realized suddenly that he was not as afraid as he ordinarily was. Something was definitely different.

A few weeks later, he was assisting another officer making an arrest. "The suspect broke free and ran," Mike says. "I tackled him, and we fell into a hole in the street, where the Con Edison crews had been digging. The suspect landed first, and I fell on top of him, making it easy to handcuff him. But the hole was too deep for us to get out. We had to wait for backup."

When extra officers arrived, they hauled the prisoner out of the hole. Then they grabbed Mike's hands and pulled him up. "Lucky that you landed on him—you could have been hurt," one officer remarked.

"Yeah," Mike murmured. Again he was filled with anxiety. Would he never be free of it? And then, near the side of the excavation, he saw two large black men wearing Con Edison helmets, smiling at him as he passed. They were the same two—he knew it! But when he looked back, they had vanished.

Over the next few months, Mike spent a lot of time thinking. He was in a unique position, he knew. He had already begun to witness to other police officers, even to people on the street, about how knowing Jesus was changing his life. Maybe God was building his confidence, so he would have both the physical and mental courage to do whatever he was asked to do. But how would he know for sure?

One afternoon Mike went into a restaurant for lunch. He had passed two diners at a table before he realized . . . He turned in amazement. There were the same two black men, both looking directly at him.

Joy flooded his spirit. "I couldn't help it," he says. "I winked at them."

Each man winked back. Mike could hardly keep from laughing out loud. He seated himself, then looked back. The table was empty.

It was the sign he had needed. From that point on, although Mike continued to have occasional anxious moments on the job, he never felt alone. Sometimes he'd sense that he was being prepared for an upcoming dangerous moment. Occasionally he would walk into angry crowds, disarm gunmen, or display sudden strength, all without being injured.

It wasn't the sort of thing one could put in a police report. But Mike understood. "I knew now that Jesus was right beside me, and would never leave me," he says. Jesus, and two very heavenly bodyguards.

Who Wondrous Things Hath Done . . .

Now thank we all our God
With hearts and hands and voices,
Who wondrous things hath done,
In whom His world rejoices.
—"Now Thank We All Our God," hymn

Bill Campbell is a member of the Lutheran Church of the Atonement in Barrington, Illinois, and loves the Lord. A friendly and gracious man, he has taught Bible study for years to people of all denominations, and has collected many miracle stories, which he shares whenever possible. Bill has lost touch with the missionary who told him the following episodes, so we will call this man Jim Jackson.

Jim and his wife, Irene, both members of a London-based Episcopal church, had worked for almost thirty years in Africa. Now

WHO WONDROUS THINGS HATH DONE . . .

they needed a new church building, so they traveled through Kenya and Uganda visiting outposts and asking for funds. Church members were generous, and the Jacksons were carrying a great deal of cash with them one evening when they set up their tent in the bush. As they built a fire and cooked their evening meal, Jim became apprehensive. There were Masai natives in this area, he knew, and an outlaw branch was unfriendly to Christian missionaries.

After supper, Irene fell asleep quickly, but Jim stayed alert, growing more nervous at every rustle. Suddenly he saw a group of Masai on the outskirts of the small clearing. They were tall, ominous. Obviously they had heard about the money he and Irene were carrying.

Warlike and holding long spears, the natives moved stealthily toward him. He and Irene would have no chance against this clan, Jim knew. What should they do?

But oddly, when the Masai reached the outer edge of Jim's camp, they came to an abrupt halt. Murmuring among themselves, they reversed direction, and inexplicably slipped away.

Jim was greatly relieved, but puzzled, too. Why had the tribe not attacked? He decided to say nothing to Irene about their narrow escape.

The following night, at a new campsite, the same thing happened. There were the men, appearing even more aggressive. Lifting their spears, they moved purposely toward Jim, then again stopped and faded away.

When the tribe reappeared on the third night, Jim could bear the tension no longer. "Get it over with!" he shouted in the Masai language. "You've got the spears, and you know we've got the money. We're ready to die for the Lord!"

The leader of the group stepped out of the darkness. "We have followed you and tried to close in on you for three or four nights," he told Jim. "But we cannot. Who are these people around you?"

"What people?" Jim demanded. "You know that my wife and I are alone."

"An unusual band in white," the chief explained. "We have counted twelve of them. They circle your fire and hold hands. They are transparent, yet they will not let us through!"

Perhaps the chief and his men had been drinking, Jim thought. But he said nothing, and once again the Masai retreated. They never returned.

Jim and Irene eventually went back to London, then visited the United States to continue fund-raising. One night Jim was invited to speak to a men's group at an Episcopal church in Long Island, New York.

There were only a handful of men there when Jim arrived. A disappointing crowd, but sometimes quality was more important than quantity. Jim gave a talk describing his new church. On impulse, he added an account of his adventure with the Masai.

The men listened, transfixed. Then one spoke up. "That's an interesting story, Reverend. By any chance, did it happen last July fifteenth?"

Jim thought. He knew he hadn't mentioned a date, or even a season. But . . . yes. "It *was* July fifteenth," he said, surprised. "How did you know?"

"I had a feeling," the other answered. "Because, as you know, we've contributed to your work, and you've always been on our prayer list."

Jim looked at the others. An awareness seemed to be dawning on each of them. Their faces bore expressions of wonder.

"On the evening of last July fifteenth, we held our weekly prayer meeting here," the spokesman explained. "During prayer, some of us had a strong sense that you and your wife were in danger."

Another nodded. "We hadn't even been thinking of you. But the feeling was very powerful, and it didn't go away. Finally we stood in a circle, joined hands, and prayed for you."

"How many were you?" Jim asked, astonished. But a quick canvass of the room had already provided the count.

"Twelve," the first man answered simply. "The same twelve that are here tonight."

The same twelve that had spiritually crossed continents, Jim realized, and brought a ring of protection where it was most needed. He would never understand *how*. But he knew *who*.

On another occasion, Jim was talking to a group of African villagers about Jesus. "The Bible says we can ask for anything in his name, and it will be done," Jim explained. The people listened politely. A few days later, the chief came to Jim. "We have decided to ask your God for something," he said.

"That's called 'prayer,'" Jim explained. "What would you like to ask?"

The chief turned and pointed to the large mountain in the distance. "Whenever we trade with the tribe on the other side," he explained, "we have to climb across that mountain. It's difficult and takes much time. We want your God to eliminate this mountain for us."

Jim stared in disbelief, his heart sinking. "I'm sorry I was ever ordained," he told Irene later that night. "Right now I have less faith than that chief does."

"Maybe God *will* move the mountain." Irene smiled. "Stranger things have happened."

Jim, however, saw no humor in the situation. He had made a promise to the chief, in God's name, using words from God's book.

Not only would he be a laughingstock when the mountain remained, but the tribe would never believe that Jesus was God's Son.

That night there was an earthquake in Kenya. The Jacksons watched, trembling, as the earth rumbled and groaned. But when the sun rose, they realized that the damage was not as great as they had feared. There was only one major change in the landscape around them.

The mountain had split. Like the parting of the Red Sea, there was now a path linking the two sides, a path perfect for two tribes who wished to trade with one another.

Jim almost fainted—before he got down on his knees.

MARVELOUS MESSAGE

And still they gaz'd, and still the wonder grew,
That one small head could carry all he knew.
—OLIVER GOLDSMITH, "THE DESERTED VILLAGE"

Julie Rose O'Donnell started life with an unexpected strike against her—cystic fibrosis, a genetic, life-threatening disease that causes progressive lung deterioration. "But even as a toddler, she never let it trouble her," says her mother, Mary Ellen. Julie was reasonably healthy during early childhood, experiencing an occasional infection, but always bouncing right back. As she grew, she learned to sew, snorkel, water-ski, perform with an Irish dance troop, and play on her school's basketball team. Her courage and spirit won her a special place in the hearts of everyone in her Riverside, Illinois, community, especially her five older brothers and sisters.

One of Julie's favorite activities was taking care of her little nephew, Nicholas O'Donnell, the son of her brother Ralph and his wife, Jane. "Julie connected to Nicky the moment he was born, and really took an interest in him," Jane says. Little Nicky was crazy about Julie, too. The pair frequently went to Brookfield Zoo, not far from their homes, and were especially fascinated with the dolphin display. They spent hours watching these "angels of the sea," and knew many by name.

"One day Julie, Mary Ellen, Nicky, and I were at the display," Jane recalls. "My mom had just returned from a trip where she had been swimming with the dolphins, and we talked about how exciting that would be."

"That's what I'm going to do someday," snorkeler Julie declared to everyone, eyes shining. "I'm going to swim with the dolphins!"

If anyone would have the spunk to do it, Julie would. But the idea seemed more unlikely as she turned twelve. At puberty, cystic fibrosis becomes more critical. By winter 1993, the disease was progressing, and routine treatments were no longer effective. Julie's physician at Loyola University Hospital in Maywood decided that a double lung transplant was Julie's best hope.

"Julie and I wore beepers during that spring and summer, waiting to be notified that lungs were available," says Mary Ellen. "The night the call came, I asked Julie how she felt about it."

"Mom," Julie said, "I wish I could say no. But it means I'll get a new chance at life, so I have to say yes."

She did. In fact, the transplant was such a success that Julie came home in only six days. Her extended family, as well as friends and neighbors—who had kept so many prayer vigils—were ecstatic. "Living with transplanted lungs is not trouble-free, and can be very difficult," Mary Ellen explains. "But Julie experienced many wonderful days of healthy breathing."

Two-year-old Nicholas, who had been especially worried, was thrilled when she could play with him again. "Now, for *sure*, I'm going to swim with the dolphins someday, Nicky!" Julie told him one day at Brookfield Zoo. And why not? Always an optimist, Julie believed her future was unlimited.

Early one October morning, however, Julie awakened looking pale. "Mom," she whispered, "I don't feel very good."

Julie's physician discovered that she had a viral infection in her blood. He hospitalized her immediately. Three days later, when the sepsis triggered acute respiratory distress syndrome (ARDS), he put her on a respirator. Worried family and friends gathered. "The doctors considered doing another lung transplant," Mary Ellen says. "They put out a call across the country, but no matching donor was available."

On the morning of October 23, 1993, Jane and Ralph got ready to go to the hospital, while Jane's father and her brother Tony stopped by to take little Nicky to Brookfield Zoo. "We knew Julie was very sick," Jane says. "But she had come through so much, we were all praying that she could bounce back again." Jane gave her little boy an extra hug as she sent him off, grateful beyond words for his robust good health.

Nicky had a wonderful morning visiting the animals, and his grandfather and uncle were relieved to see him running and jumping, hopefully unaware of everyone's worry over Julie. Suddenly, however, Nicky paused in his play. Standing completely still, he frowned as if concentrating deeply. Then he looked up at "Grandy."

"Julie's in heaven," he said.

Jane's father was startled. He hadn't mentioned Julie all morning. "What did you say, Nicky?" He glanced at his watch. Exactly 12:08 p.m.

Nicky's little face was set and serious. He would say no more. Concerned, his grandfather brought him home so his mother could calm his fears. But when Jane opened the front door, her tearful face confirmed Nicky's words. "You don't have to tell me, Jane," her father said gently. "Nicky already did."

No one knew specifically what time Julie's life had slipped away; although there were people at her bedside, no one had thought to look at a clock. But a few days later, Julie's parents received the hospital certificate with the time of death plainly marked. It was 12:07 p.m.

How had Nicky known? No one could understand it. Even stranger, the knowledge did not at all diminish his grief. For several nights, he sobbed in his crib. "Julie, I need you. Come back." No one could console him, and during the next several weeks he continued to mourn. He was so little, not even three years old, his relatives told one another. Surely he would forget soon. But it didn't seem to be happening.

Several weeks after Julie's death, Loyola scheduled a memorial service for the families whose children had died at the hospital during the previous year. Many of the O'Donnells decided to go, including Jane and Ralph. "I was hesitant about bringing Nicky, especially since I knew people would be weeping and this might upset him," Jane says. "But although Nicky never falls asleep right after dinner, that evening he did."

Ralph carried his sleeping son to the car, strapped him into his seat, then took him out and carried him to Loyola's chapel. Oddly, Nicky slept through it all. Jane was glad, for the service was indeed painful. "I guess I'm kind of a 'sign' person," she says. "I'm always hoping something will let me know that things will be all right." *Julie. How we miss you.* How they all needed some comfort, just a little reassurance that this raw grief would someday lessen, that Julie was home safe in God's arms. *Julie, send us a sign.*

After the service, Jane and Ralph put their still-slumbering toddler back into the car and headed home. A few minutes later, Nicky finally awoke. "You had a long sleep." Jane turned from the front seat to look at him. "What were you dreaming about?"

Nicky smiled. "Julie."

It was the first time he had mentioned her in days. "What about Julie, honey?" Jane asked softly, dreading his tears.

But Nicky was still beaming, as if he knew a wonderful secret. Clearly, precisely, as if he were delivering a message in words not his own, he looked directly at his mother. "Julie said to tell you," he said, "that she's swimming with the dolphins."

Dolphins? Could it be true? Jane remembered Julie's long-ago pledge, and tears filled her eyes. Home, safe, with angels of the sea, and of heaven. It was what Jane had asked, what all of them needed so much to know.

Nicky was still beaming, and now his father, Ralph, had a question. "Nicky," he asked, "is Julie happy?"

Eyes shining, Nicky threw out his arms. "I can't reach as *big* as she's happy!"

Today, the pain of loss is still hard, and faith sometimes falters. But the O'Donnells take heart in the message Nicky brought them, especially since he never again mourned Julie's loss. It's as if he was given a glimpse into eternity. And why not? "The things that seem to grown people so perplexing are usually quite simple to children," said Agnes Sanford, the noted Christian mystic. "They have not quite forgotten God from whom they came."

Nor will anyone forget Julie Rose O'Donnell, who, in her all-too-brief life, graced the paths of many. She loved well and deeply on earth, and still does so from heaven. A little child has told us so.

Janet's Vision

The light of God surrounds me;
The love of God enfolds me;
The power of God protects me;
The presence of God watches over me.
And wherever I am, God is!

—James Dillet Freeman, Unity Prayer for Protection

Marilynn Webber, author of *A Rustle of Angels*, hated to visit the doctor and had not had a checkup for far too long. One night four angels came to her in a dream. "They were not the glorious shining beings I had always imagined angels to be," Marilynn relates. "These were dressed in black, and appeared to be mourning."

Summoning up her courage, Marilynn asked them why they were so sad.

"Because," said one, "if something is not done soon, you will die."

Suddenly Marilynn was wide-awake, trembling at the vividness of the dream. It had been so real, like no other she had ever had. Was it true? Was she ill?

The next day Marilynn visited her physician. Tests showed that she had uterine cancer, usually a silent killer. "If you had not come in for a checkup when you did," he told Marilynn after her successful surgery, "I don't think we could have saved you."

The precognitive dream—showing an event before it occurs—is probably the most difficult type to understand. In some cases, like Marilynn's, the forewarned dreamer can take action, or protect herself with prayer power. At other times, it appears that nothing can be done to change the outcome. At this point, perhaps the dream or vision is God's way of preparing us so that we know that he is near, and will help us to get through whatever lies ahead.

Janet J. Corrao agrees. She was busy packing for a family vacation to Pennsylvania in August 1992 when she had an odd experience. "I heard a voice, not actually an audible voice, but somewhere in my mind," Janet says. "The voice asked me what I would do if our car were to catch on fire." A ridiculous question, Janet thought. But before she knew it, she had answered. "I'd jump out, of course."

The voice persisted. "What about your children in the backseat?"

"Why, I'd go back and get them." Janet stopped. Could she? Could she actually run through flames to rescue her little ones? Few people are called to risk their lives in such a way. What about her?

As she pondered the idea, she suddenly saw a scene, so vivid that it seemed a movie screen had rolled down in front of her. She and her husband, Joe, were sitting in the front seat of their car, and their three children were in the back. Joe was shouting at her. "Get out! The car's on fire!" Now he was leaping out from behind the wheel, wrenching open the car's back door and dragging their eleven-year-old daughter, Liana, from her seat.

Janet saw herself act on the mental screen, too. "I nodded to him, picked up something on the seat, turned around, and unlocked the doors—mine first, then the back—got out, opened the back door, unbuckled my first-grade daughter Toni's seat belt, then unhitched the three-year-old, Joey, from his car seat—he was asleep. Carrying him, I grabbed Toni and ran with her to the front of the car where there were some safety barrels, the kind they use on road construction, with fluorescent rings around them. We huddled behind the barrels as the car exploded and burned." Then the scene faded.

Janet was aghast. What a terrible thing to contemplate! And why? Gradually her pounding heart quieted, and she resumed her packing chores. She wouldn't think of the strange occurrence again.

The rest of the day passed normally. As Janet prepared dinner, however, the vision returned, and she saw the entire sequence again.

Oh God, please take it away! she heard herself praying. This was the last thing she needed at the start of a vacation.

That night Janet dreamed again and again of the event, in a bizarre series of instant replays. "The next day I told Joe about it," she recalls. "Bless his heart, he said very little, just told me to try and relax and not let my imagination get the best of me." But Janet was becoming edgy. Through that day, as she put together the final touches on their departure, the dream/vision came several times, now in a speeded-up version. Joe shouting, leaping out to grab Liana. Janet nodding, picking up something on the seat, unlocking the doors, unbuckling Toni, lifting Joey, running, hiding behind the barrels. Faster, faster! "I couldn't stop seeing it no matter how hard I tried," she says. "I thought I must be losing my mind."

On Sunday morning the Corraos started out in rainy weather, but before long, the sky cleared and the Pennsylvania mountains loomed majestic and beautiful. They arrived in Hershey safe and sound, and reached Lancaster the following Monday evening. Janet hadn't had the dream for two days. She was relieved. Hopefully the whole bizarre ordeal was over.

"But at four o'clock in the morning, I sat bolt upright in the motel bed, shaking like a leaf," Janet says. "I had had the dream again! The television was right across the room, and I seemed to be seeing that scene on the screen!" *Nod, grab something on the seat, unlock doors, unhitch Toni, pick up Joey, run to the barrels, run.* Joe awakened and tried to comfort her. "I know it was getting to him. But all I could think of was, Lord, we're so far from home. What if something *does* happen? Please send your angels to take care of us."

The following day they visited Strasburg, an Amish community, and while in a store, Janet saw a blue and white striped conductor's hat. She felt a strange urge. "We have to get that for Joey," she said. Her daughters looked at her in surprise. Mom was always telling them not to ask for souvenirs, and here *she* was, buying a silly hat for their little brother! "But as soon as we bought it, I felt very peaceful," Janet says, "as if it was meant to be."

The dream didn't come that night. Had it—mercifully—ended? Janet didn't dare to hope. But on their last morning, she turned toward their New Jersey home with a lighter heart. Rather than take the turnpike back, Joe opted for a more scenic route, through side roads and minor highways. Instead, it turned out to be a maze of stores and traffic lights and malls, which slowed their pace and confused them. Eventually they realized they were lost.

Joe was very agitated, and an ominous feeling seemed to have settled over everyone. Janet began to pray, almost urgently. Something was happening, but she felt helpless to stop whatever was going on. Suddenly Joe broke the silence. "Look out the back window, Janet. Do you see smoke?"

Janet turned. It looked like a heavy exhaust. "Maybe we got some bad gas?" she suggested.

Abruptly Joe swerved over to the shoulder. "Get out!" he shouted at her as he leaped out his side and wrenched open the back door to grab Liana. "The car's on fire!"

On fire. Janet saw blue flames whooshing past her. And suddenly she knew just what to do. Calmly she picked up Joey's new hat from the front seat, turned and unlocked both doors, got out, and opened the back door. Methodically she undid Toni's belt, unhitched her sleeping son from his car seat, while repeating the same quiet phrase: "The car is on fire, but it's all right. It's all right."

Grabbing the two small children, Janet hurried toward the front of the car, Liana running beside her. Was she dreaming now? No, there were the two safety barrels just ahead on the shoulder, with wide fluorescent bands on them, and she and the children ducked behind them. Now she could see flames dripping into a puddle under the engine. *It's going to blow up*, she thought. Where was Joe?

Joe had run toward a truck that had pulled up behind the burning car. A moment later he and the driver began throwing roadside dirt onto the flames. Soon the fire went out, and a moment later, Janet heard the sound of sirens approaching.

The truck driver, an off-duty Allendale, New Jersey, police officer, had called for aid on his car phone. But he still couldn't believe everyone was safe. "I saw your car from a half mile back, flames and smoke covering it," he told Janet as she and the children emerged shakily from behind the barrels. "I thought you were all goners."

The emergency medical techs checked everyone over for carbon monoxide poisoning. "They, too, were amazed," Janet says. "We'd had the air conditioning on, and the fumes from the smoke had filled the car. The children should certainly have been sick, if not worse. But we were all fine."

It wasn't until the car had been towed and the family brought to a hotel lobby to phone relatives that Janet had a moment to relax. And as she did, she heard a by-now-familiar voice in her mind. "See how much he loves you?" the voice asked.

The dream! She hadn't thought about it until now! "Yet, with the exception of the explosion, everything had happened in exactly the way I'd been shown. The hat on the front seat—I hadn't bought it when I'd first had the dream, so of course, I couldn't identify it. Joe's warning, unlocking the doors, picking up the children, flames all around us, and me so calm." Far from a misfortune, the dream had been a mysterious and unexplained dress rehearsal, right down to the little unimportant detail of the hat, a specific preparation so she would act decisively and remain calm.

The car was checked over several times by mechanics, but no problem was ever found, and Joe drove it safely for another year. The Corrao children experienced no fears after the episode, and were not at all reluctant to travel in cars. Janet never had the dream again, or any other premonition. And she doesn't know why this particular warning came in a dream.

"But I do believe," she says, "that if there is something you must know, the Lord will find a way to get you the message, clear and concise, with no doubt about where it came from."

He loves us, she says, that much.

ANGELIC LIFEGUARD

But if these beings guard you, they do so because they have been
summoned by your prayers.

—ST. AMBROSE, FOURTH CENTURY

Kimberly Winters McJunkin and her sister, Rachel, had learned to swim in their hometown pool in Waxahachie, Texas, and were very assured around water. So when their family visited relatives in Alabama, and the girls discovered that Mobile Bay was just behind their aunt's house, they were delighted. "The next day we loaded our swimming stuff in the car," Kimberly recalls. "On impulse, my mother added my dad's swimming trunks. My dad is not a swimmer, but occasionally he wades on the shore."

The family arrived at Aunt Elaine's house, where she, Mr. and Mrs. Winters, and a neighbor got comfortable on the beach. "Our younger brother played at the water's edge, but Rachel and I wanted to be in really deep water," Kimberly says. "We walked out into the bay."

It was a long trek. The area was quite shallow, and the girls kept going, wondering when they would be deep enough to swim. "Look!" Rachel laughed once as she turned around. "Everyone on shore looks like tiny dots!"

The adults had been talking animatedly amongst themselves, but eventually Aunt Elaine looked up and gasped. "No one ever goes out that far! The girls should come back."

"It still looks pretty shallow," Mrs. Winters observed.

"No, there's a steep drop-off somewhere out there, a ship's channel. And there are stingrays and jellyfish, too." Aunt Elaine jumped up. "Girls! Turn around!"

"Murl." Mrs. Winters turned to her husband. "Could you . . . ?" But Mr. Winters was already heading for the house to change into his bathing trunks. Surely his daughters would hear Aunt Elaine, but he would go out to them anyway.

But they hadn't. "By the time I returned to the beach, only the girls' shoulders and heads were visible," Murl says. "They were at least a half mile from shore." He plunged into the water. *Jellyfish. A sheer drop-off.* He had to get their attention. "Kimberly! Rachel!" he shouted, but to no avail. The other adults watched in fear. Their carefree conversation had long since turned into prayer.

By now, with the water over their heads, the girls were plunging into waves, skimming up and down, and having a grand time. Occasionally something brushed against their legs, but they weren't afraid. When they saw their father approaching, they were surprised. "Dad, what are you doing here?" Kimberly asked. "You never go in the deep water."

"You're a little too far," Murl called calmly. "Come closer to the beach."

The girls obeyed, Murl waded back in to shore, and all was fine. If their father seemed more thoughtful than usual that evening, none of his children really noticed.

But the following day, Murl decided to share something with his family. He had gone into the bay to call his daughters in, he reminded everyone. And then something had happened.

Murl had seen a third person in the water with the girls. At first he had assumed that it was the neighbor, and had wondered how she had gotten to his daughters ahead of him. But then he had realized that it wasn't her. This figure was a man, a young man, wearing a white T-shirt.

The man did not seem to be talking with Kimberly and Rachel, or touching them as they skimmed up and down through the waves. Instead, he was swimming *around* them, in a protective sort of arc. "At times he was between the girls, and at other times I noticed he was on one side or the other," Murl says. He'd blinked, doubting what he saw. Was it a trick of sunlight? Was he seeing double?

No, for if he was, he would be seeing two images of his daughters and two of the man as well. Further, the second image would be moving in synchronization with the first. Instead, all three figures were moving independently of one another. But who?

The man continued to swim back and forth, watching the girls intently—until Murl got just a few yards away. "By then only your heads were visible," Murl told his daughters. "When you turned at the sound of my voice, I realized that the figure had vanished."

Shocked, Kimberly thought of the brushes against her legs, the dangerous depth of the bay. What if she or Rachel had gotten a cramp, or been bitten? "In our eagerness to have fun, we had endangered our lives, and we didn't know it," she says. "But God chose this moment to reveal the fact that he was watching. And he still watches, every day, even when we aren't in trouble."

LOVE IN THE LIGHT

God's ways seem dark, but, soon or late,
They touch the shining hills of day.

—JOHN GREENLEAF WHITTIER, "FOR RIGHTEOUSNESS SAKE"

Eleanor Bickenheuser was a small-town girl from Bedford, Indiana, when—after a whirlwind courtship in 1958—she married William J. (Jerry) Westfall, then a first lieutenant in the army. Within a year, Jerry was assigned to the 503rd Aviation Company of the Third Armored Division in Hanau, Germany. Eleanor said good-bye to her family and friends, and prepared for adventure on the other side of the world.

Hanau was an obscure town known only, Eleanor says, as the birthplace of the Grimm brothers, the authors who wrote fairy tales. But during that first year, Eleanor found her new life fascinating. Nor was she as lonely as she had expected to be. "Military people have a special bond," she explains. "We become one another's families."

The Westfalls developed an especially strong friendship with Manny and Connie Guerraro, a warm, welcoming couple who shared practical information, home-cooked meals, and occasional custody of their small sons. When Eleanor became pregnant, Manny was as excited as if *he* were becoming a father again. "I'll bet it's a girl!" he told Eleanor and Jerry more than once.

However, he was never to know. In August 1961 Captain Guerraro accidentally flew his helicopter into a communications line and it exploded. He was killed instantly.

Eleanor grieved deeply. She had known that such maneuvers were dangerous, but the death of one so young—and so close—was difficult to handle. "There were other changes as well," she recalls. "Connie packed up her little boys and went home to the United States. When we lost him, we lost her and the children, too. And with the erection of the Berlin Wall, military tensions increased."

Then winter arrived—a bleak, dreary season when the sun was barely up at 9:00 a.m., and set again around 3:00 p.m. In December Eleanor gave birth to baby Nancy, setting off a fresh wave of sorrow despite the joy. Oh, why couldn't the Guerraros still be here to share in this special time? Nor could Jerry console her; a few days after Nancy's birth, he was assigned to field maneuvers and was gone for almost four months. Eleanor was left to learn about parenthood alone.

Because winter in Germany was so long and depressing, the Officers' Wives Club sponsored regular activities to keep the women's spirits up. One of these was a hat-making class. Hats were popular due to First Lady Jacqueline Kennedy's affection for them, and Mia, a woman who ran a millinery store in the nearby town of Bad Vilbel, came each week to teach the wives how to make their own. Since Mia had no car, someone always brought her and took her back, a round-trip distance of some twenty-seven miles.

One morning Eleanor received a call from the assigned driver, who couldn't pick Mia up because her children were sick. Could Eleanor take her place? Eleanor had been halfhearted about attending the class, but since she had a sitter for the baby, she agreed; perhaps the drive would lift her spirits.

It did not. "I decided to take the back-road route, which was surrounded by forests, rather than the autobahn, because I thought it would be quicker," she says. But the sun hadn't yet risen, and the skies were dark, heralding another gray, chilly day. The trees, stretching their leafless arms, seemed cheerless and brooding, and were growing right up to the road on both sides. As the kilometers sped past, Eleanor began to feel oppressed. Her thoughts replayed the recent tragic event, and sorrow again enveloped her like a blanket. Was there no end to it?

Abruptly Eleanor came up to a little rise in the road. As she crossed over the hill and started down, she blinked. Was she seeing things?

No, this was real. The entire landscape that lay ahead had been mysteriously transformed. Rather than growing close to the highway, the trees here, on both sides of the road, were set farther back. But Eleanor could still see them clearly—and despite the winter day, they were covered with leaves! What's more, the leaves seemed *golden* rather than green.

Astonished, Eleanor pulled over and stopped. "I began to realize that there was a warm glowing presence over the entire scene, despite the day's darkness," she says. "It was as if a marvelous heavenly light was illuminating all the leaves on the trees. Then the light went through me—not as a force, but more like a breeze. I felt charged with peace and energy, blessed and exalted and transformed, all at the same time."

For a few dazzling moments Eleanor basked in the majestic display. "Then I felt compelled to share it with someone," she says. "I raced on toward Bad Vilbel to pick Mia up." Perhaps the Hat Lady would know something about this magical place—why leaves bloomed here in winter, where the glorious light was coming from.

But Mia only looked in bewilderment at the excited army wife. And as the two women sped back on the same back road, Eleanor's bafflement grew. Of course, the clearing would be there—it had to be! "But we passed nothing remotely resembling it," Eleanor says. "For the entire distance back to the base, the dark leafless trees grew up to the very edge of the road." Nor, despite many subsequent trips on that road, did she or anyone else ever come across that enchanting scene again.

But Eleanor believes she received the message it sent. "To me, the golden light was reassurance from heaven. God sent it to let me know that, despite the difficult time I was experiencing, and more losses that lay ahead, he was there. And not only for me, but for all of us—in everything, even the most dismal, heartbreaking moments. I felt he was saying, 'Eleanor, get in gear. Stop grieving now because everything is fine.' And I did."

A magical, marvelous vision. Eleanor never found an explanation for it. Nor has she ever needed one. Some things should remain mysterious.

CANINE SENTRIES

Angels, where'er we go, attend
Our steps, whate'er betide;
With watchful care their charge defend,
And evil turn aside.

—CHARLES WESLEY, HYMN

Nora* doesn't want her real name used, "because I am still embarrassed at how naive I was." At that time, as a shy eighteen-year-old, she was caught up in romantic dreams. "More than anything, I wanted a man in my life," she says. "My best friend had just met someone special, and I longed for the same thing to happen to me."

Nora lived with her older brother Mark,* his wife, and their baby just outside a small Arkansas town, because it was close to her job at a shoe factory. Sharing the house were three hounds, white with large black spots, which Mark used for coon and quail hunting. The dogs were affectionate and rowdy, always jumping up on Nora, and she enjoyed playing with them. She babysat for her young nephew occasionally, and attended church every Sunday. "I believed in God and the Bible," she says. "My mother always told me that if I ever got in trouble, I should ask God for help." Nora didn't anticipate trouble of any kind—in fact, *that* was the trouble! Although her life was pleasant, it seemed to be on hold.

One day a friend introduced Nora to a handsome young man. Nora liked Peter* right away, and when he invited her out for a casual dinner, she gladly accepted. But during dinner, Peter made several suggestive comments, and Nora became apprehensive. She was relieved when he drove her back to her brother's house.

"By now it was dark, and there was a little lane leading past the house. Peter suggested we take a stroll before he left," Nora says. "I was hesitant since I knew my sister-in-law and the baby had gone to her parents' for the weekend, and my brother was out hunting. But it was a beautiful, starry night." Peter held her hand, and despite misgivings, Nora's romantic dreams took over.

However, she had made a mistake. Before they had traveled more than a few yards down the deserted path, Peter suddenly attacked Nora, pushing her to the ground. He was tremendously strong, and, horrified, Nora realized that she would be no match for him. Panic almost overwhelmed her, but then a thought flashed through her mind. God was watching her! He knew what was going on, he loved her, and he wouldn't desert her—her mother had said so.

"God, help me! Send help!" Nora cried out as she struggled. "God, please . . ." It seemed hopeless. Peter was overpowering her, but Nora continued to pray aloud. Words that she wasn't even thinking about poured forth. *God, help, help*. Suddenly, Nora felt a presence. Looking up, she gasped. Mark's three black-and-white hunting dogs, outlined in moonlight, stood over them.

Mark! Was he nearby? Had he heard her scream? But there wasn't a sound. His dogs would never leave his side, Nora knew. And these were definitely his dogs—she recognized their distinctive markings. But why had she not heard them approach? And why had they not barked and jumped upon her, as they always did?

Startled, Peter let go of her. He stared at the dogs, and the dogs stared back. One barked, once or twice, then quieted. The others stood mute, neither attacking nor retreating—just standing there, like sentries. It was almost, Nora thought, as if they understood what was going on and were looking on in eerie disapproval.

Peter got up and moved away, walking faster and faster as he headed back to his car. The dogs watched but stayed with Nora, encircling her. "You'll be all right now," they seemed to say. Shakily she rose to her feet. She *was* all right, except for her disillusionment. If it hadn't been for the dogs . . . Slowly she started up the lane toward the house, looking back to see if they were following her. But now the lane was empty. They must have returned to Mark. But why hadn't he come to her?

Several hours later Mark finally pulled his truck into the driveway. Now the dogs were barking noisily, and when they saw Nora they jumped out of the truck and leaped affectionately upon her. "Where have you been?" Nora asked Mark as she warmed up some food for him.

"The dogs and I were coon hunting over in Finch tonight," Mark told her.

Finch. It was at least fifteen miles away. "*All* night?" Nora asked, puzzled.

"We left about the same time you did," Mark explained. "We've been up in the hills ever since."

The dogs couldn't have covered a fifteen-mile stretch to be at her side. "Were the dogs with you the whole time?" Nora asked.

"The whole time, just like always."

"Then . . ." Perhaps the animals she'd seen belonged to someone else. No, Nora knew every hound in the area, and none looked quite like Mark's. And what kind of dog would be so silent, so protective?

Mark was looking at her curiously. But she would need some time to think before she could tell her brother—or anyone—about what she was beginning to believe. For if the dogs that had rescued her were not Mark's or anyone else's, then where had they come from? And who had sent them?

Today Nora is married and the mother of two. But she will never forget that night. "I think it was divine intervention," she says. Angels do come in many forms.

Always a Father

Heaven and earth are threads from one loom.

—Shaker saying

It was a brisk October morning in 1991 when Sharon Stultz set out for Pittsburgh to pick up her second car (which had broken down at a friend's house there) and tow it back to her home in Alexandria, Virginia. She had never towed anything before and was nervous, but she put the rented hitch on the back of a borrowed pickup truck and drove toward the interstate.

"Just before merging, I bowed my head and said, 'Dear Lord, please take me and bring me back, and keep me in the hollow of your hand,'" Sharon says. While she prayed, she thought of her father, a huge burly man who had always been her guardian—and her best friend. She still missed him, although he had died almost ten years ago. If Dad were here, Sharon knew, he would get the car for her, or at least go along to help. She sighed. Hopefully her father was watching from heaven and would send some added protection her way.

The trip to Pittsburgh proved uneventful, so after she hitched the car, Sharon decided to return home that same night. But by the time she reached Breezewood, Pennsylvania, it was 10:00 p.m., and she realized she had made a mistake. "Pulling the car slowed me down, and I was starting to feel the effects of the driving and the tension," she says. It was time to find a motel.

At a truck stop Sharon enjoyed a fortifying meal. But there were no rooms available. "I stopped at several motels, but no one had a vacancy," she says. By now she was almost in a panic. She couldn't imagine sleeping in the truck on the side of a road. But how could she drive safely? Slowly she pulled into traffic again. "Lord, you've been holding me in your hand and I'm grateful," she murmured. "But I need some extra help right now."

An empty stretch of road loomed ahead. Sharon continued to pray, and she passed Hagerston, Maryland, without incident. But as she approached Frederick, she felt the truck veer. She had almost driven off the highway! She *had* to stop now, before she crashed. No, she couldn't—where would she sleep? Just fifty or sixty miles more, but her eyes were heavy, so heavy. She was nodding and she wasn't going to make it.

Then Sharon felt a cool breeze brush her cheeks, and a pair of large hands come gently down over hers on the steering wheel.

It was as if someone else were taking over for her, someone safe, someone she knew. Her eyes closed completely, and she slipped into blessed rest.

Sharon awakened the next day at 11:00 a.m., fully dressed and lying in her own bed. Astonished, she leaped up and looked out at the driveway. Her *other* car was there, the one she had parked at her friend's house when she borrowed his pickup.

"Sure, the truck and your towed car are here," the friend said when Sharon phoned. "You left them here and picked up your other car early this morning, didn't you?"

She didn't know. She didn't remember *anything*. How could she have driven fifty miles, exchanged one car for another, and reached home safely without being aware of it?

But wait. A faint memory lingered, of peace, of being cared for, of large but tender hands on hers, hands that she recognized—her *father's* hands! Tears sprang to Sharon's eyes. It couldn't be. But hadn't she asked God to send her some added protection? And what more perfect choice could he make?

A few days later, Sharon met a friend in the supermarket. "Hey, I saw you towing a car on 495 late the other night," he said.

Highway 495 was the beltway around Washington, DC, her last lap home. But she had been asleep by then.

"I was wondering," the friend went on, "who was the big guy driving your truck?"

"The big guy?" Sharon asked.

"Well," he paused. "I couldn't tell for sure, but it *looked* like a guy. And yet I could see you, too, in the same seat. There was a lot of light around you, like a glow." He shrugged. "Guess it sounds pretty strange."

Not strange, Sharon thought. The pieces all fit.

"I will always be grateful to God for the privilege of being able to sense my father's presence, of knowing that Dad is still watching out for me from heaven," she says. And just in case she harbored any doubt, a recent occurrence helped dispel it.

A man who lives across the street from Sharon walks to the bus stop about the same time each morning as she does. "Our street is very dark then, and I'm always a little nervous until I get to the stop," she says. Although the neighbor had never spoken to Sharon, one morning he approached her.

"I'd give a lot to know who that man is, the one who walks behind you," he said.

"Man? What man?" Sharon asked.

"He's really big, hard to miss. And he's there every day, just following you. But when you get to the bus stop, he's nowhere in sight."

Oh, yes, he is, Sharon thought. *I can see him with my heart.*

WHEN WE ASK

Seek the Giver, never the gift. If you want something from God, then you get alone with Him, talk to Him about it.

—SANDRA PRATT MARTIN, *BITE YOUR TONGUES*

Persistent prayer is part of God's plan for helping us develop a relationship with him. And sometimes we need to pray over a long period of time so God can build up areas of faith within us that are weak and need help.

But there are also moments when the response to our prayer is so immediate—and so intimate—that we're filled with wonder at God's tender touch.

Twenty-five-year-old Eugenio Mendez was living alone in Seattle, Washington, far from his large family, grappling with the demands of a new job. He had attempted to date and make friends, but he was shy, and socializing was difficult. "Gradually I slipped into a routine of working long hours, coming home and watching a little TV, then falling asleep," he says. "Soon I was deeply depressed."

One night Eugenio stared mindlessly at the tube. If only he had a sign, something to give him confidence that his life would not always be so lonely. "God," he said aloud, "I don't think I can take much more. Please help me."

Almost immediately, Eugenio heard a soft knock. Surprised, he looked up. In all this time in Seattle, he had only had one or two visitors. He must be hearing things.

The knock sounded again, a bit more insistent. Eugenio opened the door. In front of him stood a small African American girl, holding a flower. Eugenio looked past her, expecting to see an adult. But the hallway was empty.

Eugenio looked back at the child. She had compassionate eyes, he noticed, and seemed wise beyond her age. Smiling, she held the flower out. "This is for you," she said, placing it in his hand. Then she turned and skipped down the stairs.

This is for you. Her words were as sweet as a kiss. In a moment, the yoke of despair had lifted from his shoulders, never to return. A few years later Eugenio married, and his life is now rich and full. But although he never saw the child again, he will never forget her perfectly timed heavenly message: "You are not, and will never be, alone."

Ken called the host and me on radio station KXLY in Spokane, Washington, about the day he had to pull a tractor across a mountain range. "My car's engine needed some work, but I decided to make the trip anyway," he explained. The engine sputtered and slowed, however, and Ken soon realized he needed to replace the spark plugs.

But where? It was dusk, and the highway was deserted. He was creeping along at ten miles an hour, and at this rate it would take all night to cross the range. "God, I did a stupid thing. Please get me out of this," Ken prayed.

Up ahead was a small grocery store. Ken pulled onto the shoulder of the road and went inside. The clerk was alone, and she had no spark plugs. "We've never sold them," she said, "and I don't know where you could get them at this time of night. Not without leaving the road and driving way out of your way."

Ken looked out the front window sadly. Now what? Just then a small panel truck pulled up next to his car. "The writing on the side of the truck said 'Spark Plugs,'" Ken told listeners. "Not 'Automotive Supplies' or 'Ed's Service' or anything generic. Just 'Spark Plugs.' As if it had been sent specifically for me."

Ken dashed across the highway. The truck driver had seen the parked car and wondered if anyone was in trouble. Yes, he had four spark plugs of the proper size in stock. The two men replaced the parts, and the driver took the money and drove away. Ken made it across the mountain on time—and safe.

"So often things work out just right," Ken reminded us, "and we forget that the credit might belong to someone other than ourselves."

Roland and Mary Tom Haun have a two-hundred-acre farm in central Kentucky. They are both teachers and raise Appaloosa horses as a second business. One winter evening Roland was attending a meeting, and Mary had to bring hay to the horses in the field by herself.

"It had been snowing all day and we had several inches on the ground," Mary explains. Now the wind was whipping it around. Mary loaded the tractor with bales of hay, but for some reason, she decided not to dump it in the usual spot near a fence. Instead she brought it directly to the horses where they were huddling together in the center of the field. It was a fortunate decision because, as Mary approached the herd, she saw blood on the snow. Apparently a horse had been injured. Which one, and how badly?

"I started spreading hay out for the horses, and looking to see which one was hurt," Mary said. "But it was getting darker." Finally she found him—a young stallion. Each time he took a step, blood shot out of a cut on his leg. Mary tried to catch him, but it is difficult to overtake a horse in an open field, even harder when it is eating and doesn't want to be disturbed. The stallion kept evading her, wandering among the others. Wind whipped Mary's cheeks, and she grew even more concerned. If she didn't catch him, he could bleed to death during the night.

After what seemed like a very long time, Mary started to pray. "God," she said, "I don't want to leave this horse to die. But if I don't get him into the barn, that's what will probably happen. Can you help?"

The stallion had gone all the way across the field. Suddenly, however, he stopped, turned, looked at Mary, then calmly started to walk back. He strode right through the group of horses directly toward the barn, as if someone were leading him, not stopping for even a morsel of hay. As Mary watched in disbelief, the stallion entered the barn, then turned and met her eyes, as if to say, "*Now* are you satisfied?"

Quickly Mary closed the barn door and went for help, convinced that God answers even the smallest prayer.

Thirteen-month-old Seth Beach had been born with a hole between the pumping chambers of his heart, and a recent EKG revealed that it was getting bigger. A catheterization would determine the size of the hole, and what to do next, so Seth's worried parents made the arrangements.

"My father drove to the hospital the night before the procedure to visit us," Seth's mother, Phyliss, recalls. "As he pulled into the hospital parking lot, a man in a car one space away called to Dad, asking if he had any water for his engine. Dad did, and as he poured it into the car, the man mentioned that he was visiting his wife."

Phyliss's father spoke of his baby grandson and the family's concern.

"Are you a praying man?" the stranger asked.

"I certainly am," Phyliss's father answered.

"Well then," the man replied, "when I get home I'm going to get on my knees and pray for your grandson. Expect a miracle."

Phyliss's father turned to put the water jug on the floor of his car's backseat. *Expect a miracle.* It was an unusual thing for a stranger to say. He looked up. The man—and his car—had vanished, even though the only way out of the lot was past him. And no vehicle had gone by.

He was still pondering the mystery when he arrived in Seth's room. "I think I've just met an angel," he told his daughter.

Phyliss thought Seth could use all the extra prayers possible, whether from angels or ordinary mortals. But it was not until the following day that she realized the power of the stranger's promise.

For Seth's physician could find no trace of the hole. There was only a narrowed valve, which has given this healthy child no trouble ever since.

Ten-year-old Kristy and her sisters were returning from visiting a relative, riding in the open back of their stepfather's pickup truck. Kristy was afraid of her stepfather. He had a terrible temper, and she never knew what was going to make him mad.

The truck bumped along the rutted rural road. Kristy was holding her new red jacket when a sudden gust of wind blew across the truck. Her jacket flew out of her hands. "Oh, no!" she cried, watching it rise into the air.

Her stepfather pulled the truck over. "Did something just blow out of the truck?" he asked angrily.

No one spoke. Kristy's heart began to pound. She had seen her jacket fly into the fields and disappear. It was gone forever.

Her stepfather seemed to already know. "You had better have your jacket with you when we get home," he said to her, and pulled onto the road again.

Kristy and her sisters looked around the open truck just in case, but there was nothing to see. Kristy began to cry. She was in trouble, and she would be punished. "Please God, please," she murmured. She didn't know if that was the right way to pray, but it was all she could do.

When the truck pulled up in front of the house, her stepfather got out and came around to the tailgate. "Kristy, where is your jacket?" he asked.

Kristy opened her mouth to tell him the truth. Just then, her sister grabbed her arm. "Look!" She pointed.

Lying in the middle of the truck floor, in plain sight, was the red jacket.

What goes around comes around. Roberta Eschenbaum, a farmwife living outside Miller, South Dakota, certainly knows this to be true. She had taken a quick trip into Miller one morning, and was rushing home to get the noon meal on the table for the men. As she drove, she was also keeping an eye out for her father, who lived alone and had emphysema "He didn't drive much except for the twelve miles out to our farm," she says, "so I always knew that if he needed help on the road, someone would stop." But it was still a worry for her, and she often prayed for his safety.

There was no sign of Roberta's father's car. Instead, up ahead, she saw another vehicle stopped at the side of the road, a man peering into the engine. "I was in a hurry, and although I always help people I know, this man was a stranger," Roberta says. She should have kept going. But something told her to stop, and she did.

The driver was having trouble with his battery, so Roberta drove to a neighboring farm, borrowed booster cables, drove back, and got the car going.

"This is wonderful." The driver thanked her and reached for his wallet. "Could I . . . ?"

"No payment necessary." Roberta smiled, getting back in her car. "Just return this favor by helping the next person you find stalled along a road."

"I certainly will!" The man waved as she pulled out.

Two weeks later, Roberta's father phoned, with an interesting story to tell. "I went to an auction about fifty miles southwest of here," he began.

"Fifty miles!" Roberta was aghast. "Dad, you never drive that far alone!"

"And I got a flat tire on the way home."

By now Roberta was in a panic. The area he was describing was a backcountry road with little or no chance of anyone coming by. Nor could her father have changed his own tire, weakened as he was. "What happened?" she asked.

"You wouldn't believe it. A nice motorist came along right away and changed my tire. But when I offered to pay him, he said no. Seems a woman outside of Miller had given him a battery jump two weeks ago and told him to pass on the favor. He was paying a debt to her."

Roberta felt love surrounding her like a hug. "I think God knew Dad was going to do that, and so he arranged a rescue ahead of time," she says. "I look for evidence of his presence all the time—and I always find it."

Margaret Farnaus had sung soprano in her church choir since she was a young girl. "My favorites were the traditional hymns like 'Blessed Assurance' and 'Fairest Lord Jesus,'" she says. "When I sang, all my feelings seemed to pour out. It was my absolutely favorite thing to do."

Margaret and her family eventually moved and joined a church where these songs were rarely sung. She had intended to sing in the choir anyway, but over the next several months she noticed her once crystal voice turning gravelly and hoarse. Lozenges and sprays had no effect. "I could no longer hit the high notes," she explains. "It was a painful thing to face, but my singing days were apparently over."

Margaret had become friends with a woman, Myrtle, who eventually developed cancer. Margaret visited her friend regularly in the hospital, even after Myrtle fell into a coma. On Myrtle's birthday, Margaret slipped into the room and gazed at her unconscious friend. Myrtle was hooked up to tubes now, and Margaret sensed her life ebbing away. If only they could communicate! She put her hand on Myrtle's arm. "God," she prayed, "help me to help her."

Unbidden, the comforting words to "God Will Take Care of You" came to Margaret's mind. She hadn't sung that song in years. She didn't remember all the lyrics anymore, and her voice was so terrible now. But if Myrtle could hear her, perhaps the words would bring comfort. Bending over the bed, Margaret began to sing. Quietly at first, then with growing confidence because, in astonishment, she heard her own voice as high and sweet as it had been so long ago.

How could this be? Margaret didn't know, but still singing, she sat down next to Myrtle and took her hand. Then she began another favorite, "What a Friend We Have in Jesus." She was remembering *all* the verses, she realized, with no hesitation or groping. Her heart lifted with joy. She kept singing.

All afternoon, with only one woman as her audience, Margaret gave a very special concert. At least forty of her favorite hymns, with all the words to all the verses, came to her mind, and she sang every one. And her voice! It was as clear as crystal, true and lovelier than ever before. A stranger glancing into the room might have seen a patient unresponsive and asleep, but Margaret sensed that she *was* making contact, that somehow Myrtle knew she was not alone, that a friend had brought her a special gift for her final birthday.

Margaret was still singing several hours later when one of Myrtle's bedside machines buzzed. Myrtle took one breath, then relaxed. Nurses came running, but there was nothing to be done.

Margaret left the hospital in sorrow, yet strangely exalted as well. "I felt as if I had experienced some connection with heaven," she says. And there was also the wonder of her vocal recovery to ponder.

But when Margaret attempted to sing at home, she realized that her voice had returned to its former hoarse state. Nor could she remember the titles, much less the lyrics, of even a few of the songs she had sung so effortlessly on this blessed day.

Eventually Margaret went to a specialist and discovered that she had Sjögren's syndrome, an immune system disorder that takes moisture out of the body, rendering eyes and mouth dry, and the throat hoarse and gravelly. There were treatments Margaret could take, but no cure. Nor did the condition spontaneously improve. There was no way Margaret's voice could have reverted to its past perfection, not even temporarily. No way at all.

Unless the heavenly hosts were busy that day, and pressed an earthly angel into service to send a soul into paradise—on wings of song.

MIRACLE MAN

Vision is the art of seeing things invisible.

—Jonathan Swift, "Thoughts on Various Subjects"

Mickey Robinson grew up in suburban Cleveland in the fifties, in a typically middle-class home. "We went to church and I had a 'head knowledge' of God," Mickey says, "but I don't remember knowing anyone who had a personal relationship with Jesus. I didn't know this was important."

Mickey grew into a handsome, talented young man, with many friends. At eighteen he talked his way into a flashy job in a stock-broker's firm, which promised a career in which he could pursue the pleasures of his choice. Gradually he became a skydiving addict. "The only thing that mattered in life was jumping out of airplanes," he recalls. "No amount of money or time was too much to spend on it, and I soon became a professional. If someone had told me that I had an idol, or that skydiving was my god, I'd have considered them crazy. But your god is whatever is most dear to you—and even though I had a girlfriend and was planning to get married, I was 100 percent committed to this."

Mickey seemed to have the perfect life—by day a successful young businessman, by night a wild child of the sixties, experimenting with drugs and alcohol, and apparently enjoying it all. No one guessed that, deep inside, he battled feelings of unworthiness and fear, emotions that had plagued him all his life. "I thought I was in complete control," he says, "yet I hungered constantly for love, acceptance, and peace."

On a hot summer evening in August 1968, Mickey joined four friends for some skydiving. He and the others climbed aboard a brand-new Piper Cherokee, adrenaline already flowing. The plane cleared the runway and rose into the air at an unusually steep angle. Then, suddenly, silence! Horrified, Mickey realized that the plane's engine had failed.

"That's it!" the pilot shouted. "We're going down!" Plunging at two hundred miles per hour, the plane spun, cartwheeled, and slammed into the ground. Mickey fell forward, hitting his face. Gasoline splashed everywhere, and flames erupted.

Panic-stricken, the others crawled out of the wreckage. But Mickey couldn't follow—his leg was caught in a hole where the wing had been, and he was on fire from head to toe. The fourth skydiver looked back, saw Mickey and the pilot, who was trapped in his seat, and ran back into the blazing aircraft. His first attempts to free Mickey were fruitless, but he kept trying.

"Eventually he dragged me out, threw me on the ground, and rolled me around to put the fire out," Mickey says. "But it continued to reignite. When the rescue workers arrived, they expected to find a dead man."

Mickey had sustained third-degree burns on over one-third of his body, and doctors believed he had no chance for survival due to the complications that most surely would occur. It appeared that they were right, for during the following traumatic weeks, Mickey's weight dropped from a muscular 167 to 90 fragile pounds. His bones were exposed through open sores; ulcers and internal bleeding developed. Part of his esophagus was so scarred he could not even drink water. He was blind in his right eye, and one hand would probably have to be amputated. His temperature soared to 105 degrees, the nerves died in both his legs, and his feet curled up like claws. It took two hours each day just to change his bandages. His fiancée deserted him, and one specialist noted in his chart, "There is nothing I have to offer this young man."

Mickey drifted in and out of consciousness, aware that he—a superhero—had been reduced to complete helplessness. Desperate and lonely, he began to cry out to God. "I'm sorry," he whispered over and over, barely remembering how to pray. "Please forgive me. Please give me another chance."

One night Mickey felt his body shutting down. Was this what it felt like to die? Suddenly his hospital room vanished, and he experienced "my inner man coming out of my physical body. Immediately I became aware that the spiritual world is the real world. I also had an awareness of eternity, a complete absence of time—no one had to explain it to me. I just knew that I knew that I knew. I was traveling somewhere and had no control over it. It was awesome!"

Drawn into an intensely spectacular spiritual realm, Mickey was filled with wonder as he approached a door, with a beam of the purest white light shining through it from the other side. It was emanating from God, and he knew that the source of that light was the Source of *all* life.

Then, as Mickey watched in horror, the door began to close! "A great darkness started to surround me, and the meaning became clear—if this door closed completely, I would be cut off from this light forever."

No! "God, I want to live!" On the edge of eternity, with the darkness almost complete, Mickey cried out, "I am sorry. *Please* give me another chance!"

Instantly the glory of God overshadowed him. "Like liquid gold, it was everywhere—over me, under me, around me, vibrating through me. I felt all of God's authority, all of his power and his love. I knew now that I would never die, that I would always be comforted and cared for."

Then in front of him, almost like watching a big-screen TV, Mickey saw images. "Days, weeks, years went by, all connected together—not just one day here and there. I saw myself greeting people I never knew, as if I did know them. I saw places where I'd never been. I saw myself doing some dumb things, things I shouldn't do." There was a beautiful blond woman whom he did not know. He saw himself walking with her through a pasture. There were familiar people, too, friends from the drug scene, still shooting up. "Their faces were horrible, and I realized that I was seeing their future."

The vision ended, and the Lord told Mickey he was coming back to earth. "He did not speak in a language like I'm using now," Mickey explains. "The knowledge and awareness just came to me. I said, 'No, I don't want to leave,' but when God says something, guess what?"

Although his family and physicians continued their worried vigil, Mickey knew his near-death experience had been a turning point. He continued to ponder its significance as, during the next several years, he underwent over seventy-five operations. A cornea transplant that shouldn't have been successful gave him back his sight after five years of blindness in one eye. Plastic surgery somewhat restored his face, and physical therapy helped him regain movement. His left leg, in a brace and completely unresponsive, suddenly began to work again. He met a beautiful blond girl, who looked vaguely familiar, and after they married and moved to their first home—on a farm—Mickey realized where he had seen her before.

Far more important, however, was Mickey's inner transformation. God had removed all the things that were important to him—his physical prowess, his friends, his self-image—and put him into situations where God's strength was the only power available. Gradually Mickey saw that on his own, he could do nothing. But with God, his future was unlimited.

Today Mickey Robinson is a director of Prophetic Christian Ministries Association, and lives with his wife and four children in Franklin, Tennessee. He is able to run, snow-ski, ride horses, and, yes, even skydive. And his speaking ministry takes him all over the world, where he shares the reality of God's power to transform, with himself as a prime example. Near-death experiences, even miracles, won't change a person's heart, he believes. Only surrendering to God's will can do that. It isn't easy. But Mickey recommits himself each day.

"God looked down when I was in that darkness, and said, 'How would you like to make a deal? You trade in your life, and I will give you mine,'" Mickey says. "I think I got the better end of that."[7]

Those Who Wait upon the Lord

God has no favorites. He blesses all equally, but chooses everyone for a different work.

—Joseph Girzone, *Joshua*

When Keith and Karen Parker married in 1979, their future seemed bright. Karen had a fulfilling job as a systems analyst. Keith was a naval flight officer, flying in his favorite plane, the F-14 fighter jet. Keith loved the navy. If all went well, he would be a navigator for twenty years, retire at age forty-two with a pension, and then begin another career. In the meantime, there would be a nice house, and children. "We had everything planned," Karen explains.

But things didn't go according to schedule. In 1986 the navy sent Keith for his master's in aeronautical engineering, and the couple rented a beautiful cabin overlooking the Pacific Ocean in Monterey,

California. But no babies arrived to fill the empty rooms. Increasingly worried, Karen visited a physician about her infertility. He put her on a drug. Nothing happened.

After Keith's graduation, the couple sustained another disappointment. There were no open slots for him in any of the navy's F-14 squadrons. There *was* a job at the Naval Air Test Center in Lexington Park, Maryland, flying a remote-powered vehicle off battleships. Keith took it, although it would be three years before he'd have another chance to fly in his beloved F-14. Karen wasn't enthused. She had expected a transfer, "but this area was a rural community. It didn't even have a shopping mall. And I hated to leave my job and so many good friends," she says.

Later, however, she realized there was a strong plus about Lexington Park, Maryland. It was just a two-hour drive away from Bethesda, where the navy's own infertility clinic is located.

The movers had barely unloaded the Parkers' possessions when Karen scheduled an appointment with one of the top infertility physicians at Bethesda. "I went through all the routine tests, all the workups," she says. "I made two trips a month for almost two years." Nothing was working, but she *was* getting the best care any patient could—and because her husband was in the navy, she was getting it all at no cost to them.

"We weren't the churchgoing kind, and our faith wasn't very strong during those years," Karen says. "My infertility was so hard to understand. We would hear about abortions, child abuse, throwing newborns away in trash cans, leaving them to die. I guess I will never understand it. But I didn't blame God. I started praying for a baby, and I asked others to pray, too."

In the meantime, Keith was giving the Lexington Park job his usual 110 percent. But Karen knew he was longing to return to the F-14. It was hard to hope they would leave Maryland and the clinic—if they did, her chances for motherhood would decrease dramatically. But they both looked forward to Keith's next transfer.

But when the orders finally came, the Parkers received another blow. Due to budget cutbacks, and the downsizing of all F-14 squadrons, Keith would be discharged from the navy at the end of January 1991.

"It felt like a kick in the stomach," Karen recalls. "The navy had spent over a million and a half dollars on Keith's training, plus his master's degree, and now they didn't need him?"

Keith was in anguish. Leaving the navy . . . all their plans, their dreams. He had never anticipated this happening. But he pulled himself together and began looking for a job. "Since both our families lived in Texas, I concentrated my search there," he says. "As long as we *had* to move, we might as well be near them." Becoming parents seemed all but impossible now. But Karen continued her clinic visits.

In late November 1990, while Keith was job hunting in Texas, Karen glanced at her calendar. Hmmm. She left her office, bought a home pregnancy test, and brought it back to the ladies' room. A faint, very faint reading. Was it *positive?* "Dana!" Karen ran to a coworker's office. "Look!"

Dana was excited, too. "But just to be sure, why don't you get another kit for tomorrow morning?" she suggested.

On the way home, Karen bought a double kit. (The druggist, who had earlier sold her the single kit, looked quite confused.) The next day, a test at Bethesda confirmed what Karen already knew: her prayers had been answered.

Pregnant. She thought she would explode with joy. And Keith! She hadn't seen him this happy since before their transfer. Soon he found a job with a company in Fort Worth, and the couple bought a home and happily moved back to Texas. Karen's pregnancy was uneventful, and one of its nicest side benefits was reuniting with her beloved father. "He lived just a few miles away. We'd always been close, and we made it a point to go for a walk every day," she says. The Parkers' plans had taken a detour, but everything was back on track now.

Katelynn Leigh was born on August 13, 1991, "the happiest and the most terrifying day of my life," Karen says. Happy because their longed-for child was here at last. Terrifying because, after Katelynn had gone through the mandatory blood test to screen for PKU and a variety of other health problems, their pediatrician came to their room wearing a serious look. "There's a problem with the baby," she told them. "Her test came back positive for CAH—congenital adrenal hyperplasia. I'd like you to take her to Cook-Fort Worth Children's Medical Center tomorrow to see an endocrinologist."

Shocked, Karen and Keith heard only a portion of the doctor's words. They had never heard of CAH, but it sounded serious. After all their tests, the praying and planning, the miracle pregnancy—now a less-than-perfect child! It was yet another unexpected setback.

During the following twelve days that the baby spent in the Cook-Fort Worth hospital, while doctors worked to get Katelynn's CAH under control, Karen and Keith learned about this rare genetic disease. "Simply put, the adrenal glands do not work properly," Karen explains. "Adrenal glands control hormones, and one hormone controls body fluids. CAH babies don't have this hormone, so their bodies can dehydrate in a matter of days." Typically, permanent damage is done to newborns' kidneys, heart, and brain—in fact, they can even die—before anything is known to be wrong with them. Other side effects can also occur.

Then the Parkers learned something else. Texas is one of only two states that test for CAH as part of newborn screening. "If Katelynn had been born almost anywhere else in the country," Karen says, "she probably would have died."

Today Katelynn is happy and active. She roller-skates, dances, and takes medication—just like many other normal children. Yet her parents believe that she, and the conditions surrounding her existence, are nothing less than a miracle of God's perfect timing.

For although Keith and Karen had regarded their setbacks as negatives, these things were really positives, when viewed with spiritual vision. "It took Keith being sent to a totally different navy job to get us to the infertility clinic," Karen explains. "It took Keith being discharged from the navy to get us back to Texas, where the baby would get the immediate medical help she needed. And we didn't fully lose the navy either. Keith is a lieutenant commander in the reserves." There was even something consoling in the timing of Karen's father's sudden death, just after Katelynn's first birthday. For if the Parkers hadn't moved to Fort Worth, Karen realized, her dad would never have been able to give her the support she needed, and to see his granddaughter thrive.

"Katelynn is the sunshine of our lives," Karen says today. "Because of her I've become a stronger Christian. I know that she needs more than I can teach her. Now we enjoy going to church and praising the Lord. And I wonder if all of these events were meant to push me toward him."

Sometimes it's hard to see God's plans, for our own so often get in the way. But those who "wait upon the Lord" do learn an eternal truth. His timing is always perfect. He is never late.

WONDER AT THE WELL

Oh, we're standing on holy ground,
And I know that there are angels all around . . .
—"WE'RE STANDING ON HOLY GROUND," HYMN

Duuring the Depression, Robbie and Tom Douglas, the parents of two small girls, lived in a two-room house behind Robbie's father's farm. Like many others, their tiny community of Daysville, Tennessee, was going through hard times. Tom worked construction and felt fortunate to have a job, although each day he had to walk five miles up the side of a mountain to the road-building site, and then down again at night.

"We managed," Robbie recalls, "but the hardest part was not having water in our house." Wash water was available in a nearby creek. But to get what they needed for drinking and cooking, one of them had to walk three hundred yards up a hill and through a gate to a spring in a pasture. There they would fill and carry two-and-a-half-gallon buckets back to their little dwelling. The first supply was not always enough for the day's use either, so usually someone would have to make the trip again.

"It took a lot of time and was very tiring, especially since if Tom or I was alone, we'd have to take our little girls back and forth, too," Robbie explains. But she frequently thanked God for what they had. After all, he had provided them with a job and shelter, no matter how modest, when many had nothing at all. So although she didn't specifically pray about their water woes, "I knew God realized this situation was very hard for us."

One Saturday Robbie took their daughters to visit up at the farm, while Tom worked in the vegetable garden. Hearing a noise, he looked up to see a tall man standing in the front yard. The stranger wore black pants and the whitest shirt Tom had ever seen. "Good morning," the man called across the plants. "I'm very thirsty. Could you give me a drink of water?"

Tom stood up slowly, thinking about their precious supply. Sharing it would require another exhausting trip up to the well later. But the stranger looked hot and tired. "Would you like something to eat, too?" Tom asked.

"Just water," the stranger answered.

Tom went into the house to the container, then realized that this water would be stale by now, good enough for washing but not for a thirsty guest. He came back out on the porch. "Sir, please sit here and rest," he said. "I'm going to get some fresh water for you."

The stranger smiled. "I'd appreciate that."

Tom grabbed a bucket, climbed the hill, returned shortly with his precious cargo, and filled a tall glass. The man drank deeply. "This is wonderful water," he said, "but it's too bad you have to go so far to get it."

Tom poured him another. "It's hard, but we have many other blessings."

The stranger smiled and left a few minutes later. Tom watched him walk down the highway toward Daysville. He was beginning to wonder about the man. How had he appeared so noiselessly in the yard? And *why*? This was an isolated area; few people ever stopped by. And what could account for this unusual feeling of peace, a feeling, Tom realized, that had come upon him as soon as he'd seen the stranger?

Soon Robbie and the girls came home, and Tom, still intrigued, decided to go to Daysville's general store. The stranger would certainly have stopped there; perhaps he was still talking to the men who hung about, gossiping and exchanging news about possible jobs. But when Tom reached his destination, he had a surprise in store.

"What man?" His friends looked puzzled. The town was so small that a stranger *couldn't* escape notice. But no one had seen him. "You're the only person who's come down that road in a long time, Tom," they all insisted. Tom felt certain they were right.

About two weeks later, Daysville experienced a heavy rain, and water began seeping out of the ground about thirty feet from Tom's house. After the ground had dried, however, the little trickle remained. Mystified, Tom went back and forth for the next several days, looking at the wet spot. Finally he got his shovel. "I'm going to find out what's going on out there," he told Robbie.

He had barely broken the surface when water flowed, bubbling from an unseen source. "Robbie, come quick!" Tom called. He had found a new spring—one that was right where the stranger had stood.

"It was the end of our long trips up to the pasture, because the spring was one of the best ones around," Robbie says. "It never went dry, and it remained during the entire time we lived in that house." A short time after the Douglases moved, however, another heavy rain came, and the spring disappeared as spontaneously as it had arrived.

Robbie and Tom never doubted the source of that spring. They had given a cup of water in his name, and had been blessed abundantly in return.

TOGETHER AT LAST

Death is not lonely. . . . Those who have died before us, or some spiritual beings, will be companions on our journey.

—MAGGIE CALLANAN, *FINAL GIFTS*

To everyone who knew him, Michael J. Caldwell of Pleasant Hills, California, was a special man. He was sickly, in and out of hospitals most of his adult life, but his health problems never kept him down. He'd bounce back, enjoying his family, his job, and community service with a zest most would envy.

The only time his daughter, Kathleen, had ever seen Michael mourn was when his younger brother, Frank, died suddenly in 1977. "Dad had grown up near New York in an area called Indian Harbor, but he never spoke much about his childhood, and I got the idea that it was a difficult one," she says. "But I knew that he and Uncle Frank were very close. The sight of Dad sitting in his rocking chair and weeping over his brother's death was one I'll never forget."

As his youngest child, Kathleen was especially close to her father. That was why, when he phoned her on December 3, 1991, and asked her to take him Christmas shopping, she knew something was up. "Because of his illnesses, he no longer drove," Kathleen explains. But like many men, Michael never shopped for any holiday in advance. "Dad," Kathleen teased him, "aren't you a little early? After all, you've got almost three weeks!"

Michael's answer was significant. "No, I haven't," he said slowly. "I need to do it now."

They shopped the next day, Michael picking out an especially beautiful gift for his wife, and insisting Kathleen choose something special for herself, too. A few nights after the excursion, he called his entire family to his house. "It was very touching," Kathleen recalls. "He took each one of us aside, and told us something he especially loved about us." Her father was impatient because he couldn't get a tape recorder to work. "I fixed it for him, and when it was time to leave, he walked me outside, and stood waving at me until I drove over the hill. He had never done that before." That night Michael stayed up late, recording his life story for his three-year-old grandson, Andrew.

Thus it was almost anticlimactic when Kathleen received a phone call the next day telling her that her father had been found at home in a coma, a things-to-do list near him, with almost every item checked off. He was now in the hospital, and the family gathered at his bedside.

However, although Michael's condition was serious, he rallied and regained consciousness. Several family members assumed he would be coming home as he always had before, after bouts such as this. Kathleen's mother even rented a hospital bed and other supplies. But Kathleen had an odd feeling about it.

"That night I stayed over at Mom's," she recalls. "I used Dad's comforter on the bed. I wanted to feel as close to him as I could." Eventually she lapsed into a dream.

In the dream two little boys were playing on the bank of a large body of water. The younger began to run and called over his shoulder to the boy behind him. "Mikey!" he shouted. "Hurry! Catch up to me!"

The older boy ran faster, trying to reach the younger. "Frankie, wait!" he called.

Mikey. Frankie. Within the dream Kathleen suddenly knew that the boys were her uncle Frank and her father. They were the only ones who had ever used those nicknames for each another.

It seemed as if Mikey would not reach Frankie. "Wait!" he shouted again. And then, somehow, the two were together. Holding hands, they ran happily alongside a huge house on a hill. Kathleen had never seen the house before. It was tall, surrounded by a stone wall, and overlooked the water. The boys raced in front of the house, laughing and shouting. They disappeared, and Kathleen awakened.

"Then I knew," she says, "that my father wasn't going to rally this time. Uncle Frank had come for him, and Dad was going to be with his brother in heaven."

Michael was alert for another day, smiling and peaceful, still telling everyone how much he loved them. He was happy and yet distracted, as if part of him had already left the bonds of earth. That evening he died.

During the following year, Kathleen felt an insistent pull to go east and retrace her father's roots. Surely her cousins there would know more about the "Indian Harbor house," as her father had called it. In December of 1992 she finally made the trip. Her large Irish clan was happy to see her, and after visiting for a while, she broached the subject with a cousin. "I want to see where Dad grew up," she told him.

"Then you shall," he promised.

They went on the following day to Greenwich, Connecticut, to a spot on Long Island Sound. "This is Indian Harbor," her cousin explained.

"But where?" Kathleen looked out over the blue water, and her heart seemed to stop. There was the house, the exact house she had seen in her dream! Huge, overlooking the water.

"It's not a residence anymore," her cousin was saying, pointing. "But that's the place where your father lived." Kathleen remembered the high stone wall, the long side yard where the two little boys had run. Everything was exactly as she had seen it in her dream. But she had never been here before. Nor had she known of this house or ever seen a photo of it.

"I feel that through my dream, my father and my uncle sent me a message from heaven that they are together and happy," she says today. "In fact, they are still sending messages. My little nephew Andrew dreams about his Papa all the time, even though he is really too young to remember him. And some of my cousins also have had visions of both men."

Once Kathleen dreamed she was in church. On the altar was her father, radiant in full vestments, holding up a chalice—the symbol of life. "My father will never be gone as long as we remember him," she says. "And I believe he will keep coming at special moments, to bring us comfort and to let us know he is still near."

GUARDIANS IN THE JUNGLE

Whether you think of us or not, we are with you,
O Baptized, in the uncompromising and definitive way
willed by God:
Always, always.
Never distracted, never on vacation.
—LUIGI SANTUCCI, *CAIN'S ANGEL*

Stories of wartime angel sightings abound. George Washington allegedly saw an angel at Valley Forge. An often-told World War I event involved the Angels of Mons and the White Cavalry, white-robed beings who rode among the British troops and stopped the advance of the German armies. After Israel's Six-Day War, a story circulated about a convoy of jeeps carrying Israeli soldiers being waved onto a side route by two men whom no one saw except those in the lead vehicle. When troops went back to examine the main road, they discovered it was heavily mined.

Were angels active in Vietnam, too? Quang Nguyen is sure of it. In 1947, when Quang was a teenager, his uncle offered to send Quang and his own son to Paris to study to become wireless operators. So Quang left his wealthy family in North Vietnam and joined his relatives in Saigon. While waiting to go to Paris, Quang attended a school run by the Seventh-day Adventists. He learned English, attended a Bible class, and eventually converted to this faith.

When Quang's uncle heard about Quang's conversion, however, he was furious, and he threw his nephew out of his house. By now civil war had broken out in North Vietnam, so Quang could not return home. The Adventists took him in, let him sleep on a classroom floor, and gave him work to do.

"This was quite a change for a boy raised in luxury," Quang says, "but I decided that if Jesus, the Son of God, hadn't minded doing manual labor, why should I?"

The church people were very good to Quang, and he saved enough money to go to Singapore, and later Bangkok, where he became a lab technician. Eventually he won a scholarship to the United States to study medicine.

But by that time, the Adventist church in Saigon had asked Quang to help them start a hospital there. "They had been so kind to me that I could not refuse," Quang explains. He worked with the doctors and learned a lot, but by the time he felt he could leave for the United States, the Vietnamese government wouldn't give him a visa. Instead, Quang became the hospital's administrator.

During these years, Vietnam's long-fought civil war had inflicted great damage on the country. Now the United States stepped up its involvement, no longer acting simply as advisors, but sending troops as well. Fighting intensified.

A few hundred miles to the north of Quang's hospital in Saigon was a resort town called Da Lat. Beyond the town, farther into the mountains, lived some primitive tribes who spoke only their own dialect and wore nothing but loincloths. A few had become acquainted with the Seventh-day Adventists in Da Lat, and the church people had taught them the Vietnamese language as well as Christianity. Those natives had converted other villagers to this new religion.

Now, as war escalated, these tribes were hard-hit. Communist soldiers burned their houses, destroyed their crops, and killed and wounded many. Tragically, they were effectively sealed off from help because the route to them was too dangerous. "The Vietcong kept troops in the jungles to kill any foreigners they spotted," Quang explains. Travelling into this remote area would be madness.

But when people at the Saigon hospital heard about it, they knew someone had to bring help to the villagers. Four volunteered— the American president of the mission, an Australian physician, a

Norwegian nurse, and Quang as interpreter. The Vietnamese pastor of the church in Da Lat decided to join them, too.

"No one has ever tried this," one doctor objected. "You will be killed."

"No," one of the five answered slowly. "God will send protection for us." The others nodded. They all felt the same—the journey was somehow blessed.

First they prayed together. Then they packed a van with much-needed food, seeds and grain for planting, and medical supplies, and drove it to Da Lat. There they met a group of perhaps thirty natives, who had come to carry everything the rest of the way, since the jungle trails could not accommodate a van.

"We set off, and walked for ten hours through the mountain wilderness," Quang recalls. "The five of us certainly knew what extreme danger we were in. There was little doubt we were being watched by the Vietcong, and we expected to be stopped." Other missionaries, they knew, had ventured into this area and had never been seen again. The Vietcong had no mercy on those who invaded their territory.

They reached the village safely. However, the natives confirmed their suspicions: a unit of about twenty enemy soldiers was nearby. They were heavily armed, looking for hidden guns or radios, and had probably watched the procession all through the jungle. It was just a matter of time before they emerged from the brush and arrested everyone.

Quang and the others weren't sure such a thing would happen. Hadn't they felt protected since the beginning of their journey? Hadn't they "prayed without ceasing," as the Bible instructed? They decided to bathe and rest. "We walked to a cold mountain stream," Quang says, "but as we stood in the refreshing water, the villagers came running in alarm. Behind them were Vietcong soldiers."

Grimly the Vietcong ordered the missionaries to get out of the water and stand at gunpoint. Then the soldiers ransacked their possessions, looking for radio equipment, ammunition, or anything that would indicate a connection with the government. They found nothing. Frustrated, one of the soldiers looked up. "Where are the others?" he demanded.

"Others?" Quang answered. "Do you mean the tribesmen?"

"Not them," the soldier barked. "The others in your group."

"There are no others," Quang explained. "Only the five of us."

"Not five. Ten!" The soldier was adamant, and his men nodded. "You come with us—now!"

Quang's heart sank. It was almost dark, and he was sure that he and the others were being taken away to be quietly murdered. But there was nothing to do but follow. "Tell the hospital what happened to us," he advised the stricken townspeople. Then he and the others began, once again, to walk.

Eventually they reached a campsite belonging to the Vietcong. Instead of shooting them, however, the soldiers gave them food and sat down around them. And the story emerged.

As Quang and the others had suspected, the enemy had stealthily followed them and their bearers all day long, planning to shoot them before they reached their destination. But the soldiers had not fired because of "the other five"—tall people, dressed in radiant white, who walked alongside the missionaries through their entire journey. The soldiers had been fascinated with these glowing strangers and could not stop looking at them. "Where did they go?" one asked, mystified.

Quang knew. What else could account for the strange feeling of peace, of safekeeping, that had accompanied them from the start? But how could he explain angels to these men?

After leaving the soldiers, the missionaries completed their job and returned to Saigon without incident, to the amazement of everyone who heard of their perilous trek. Quang eventually married an American and now lives in Florida. No one ever found a trace of the mysterious jungle guardians, but he believes they are still on the job.

TRIUMPH IN THE SKY

*Two things fill my mind with ever-increasing wonder and awe . . . the
starry heavens above me and the moral law within me.*

—IMMANUEL KANT

Dallas Chopping grew up around airplanes. As a two-year-old
he sat on his pilot-father's lap, wearing earphones and "flying." While other teenage boys saved for automobiles, young Dallas
bought a plane instead. So when he became senior flight captain
for a mining company in Casper, Wyoming, he was right where he
wanted to be.

In the spring of 1987, Dallas received an unusual assignment.
One of the company's engineers, Michael Stevermer, and his wife,
Sandi, had an eight-month-old baby needing a liver transplant. Little
Benjamin had been born with biliary atresia, and had already gone
through several unsuccessful surgeries designed to buy him some
"growing time" until a donor liver could be found. "There are very

few infant organs available," Sandi Stevermer explains. "Fifty percent of babies die while waiting for a transplant."

Now a transplant was Benjamin's only remaining chance for life, and he was on waiting lists at hospitals in Omaha and Pittsburgh, places specializing in infant transplants. The Lutheran Brotherhood, a fraternal organization that raises funds for transplants and other needs, had conducted several benefits to cover costs that would be uninsured, and the people of Wyoming had been generous. Everything was in place—except the journey itself. Because the Stevermers lived in such a remote area, it was doubtful they could get an immediate commercial flight to *any* medical center, especially within the short window of time necessary for surgery to proceed (usually seven to eight hours after a donor organ became available). Nor could the weather be counted upon; when Michael and Sandi had taken Benjamin to Denver for an evaluation a few months earlier, they had almost missed their flight due to heavy snow.

"The Stevermers are wearing pagers now, waiting for a call from one of the hospitals," the company's chief executive officer told Dallas's flight department, "and if one comes, we're authorizing you to use our aircraft—or to do anything else necessary—to get them where they need to go."

Dallas seldom flew east of the Mississippi, but it didn't matter—surgery would surely take place in Omaha, since it was so much closer. However, more than six months passed with no request from the Stevermers. Dallas had almost forgotten about them when, as he worked in his garage late on a fall afternoon, the phone rang.

"There's a liver for Benjamin in Pittsburgh," an emotional Michael Stevermer told him. "Can we get there?"

"I'll meet you at the airport right away." Dallas hung up. Pittsburgh! So much farther than he'd expected, and he didn't have the necessary charts. Maybe the company jet could get them there in time. However, when Dallas phoned his flight scheduler, he discovered that the jet was in use, and the only plane available was a small turboprop. It was not nearly fast enough, and would require a stop for refueling, using up more valuable time.

Worse, the weather forecasts looked ominous. Not only would he be flying into strong headwinds, but there were thunderstorms over Chicago and snow predicted for Pittsburgh.

The whole venture was starting to unravel. He couldn't start out on a journey he knew he couldn't finish. Dallas thought of his own two toddlers. How would he feel if *their* lives depended on others?

No, he wouldn't give up before he'd even tried. He frowned, deep in thought. Maybe he could *start* with the turboprop, and transfer the Stevermers to a faster plane somewhere along the route.

Dallas made a few phone calls from home, trying to locate a charter jet, but he had no luck. He would try again en route. Heading to the airport, he soon lifted Lifeguard 205—with its precious three-passenger cargo—into the sky.

The Stevermers were too absorbed in the immediate situation to realize how concerned Dallas was. "The call from Pittsburgh had actually come in at three-thirty, but I had lost time trying to locate Michael out in the field," Sandi says. "The neighbors had rushed to help me pack and drive me to the airport, where I met him. We couldn't give Benjamin anything to eat or drink, and he was cranky before he fell asleep on the plane. I had never met the crew, and I was distracted with everything that had gone on, so I had no idea that we might not make it to Pittsburgh in time." Exhausted, Sandi prayed as she had done from the beginning of her baby's ordeal: "Lord, I can't put Ben through much more. If you're going to take him, do. I put him completely in your hands." Then she fell into a much-needed sleep.

In the cockpit, however, things were not as calm. "First, the copilot and I couldn't find a charter jet for a transfer," Dallas recalls. "Next, Mike mentioned that Pittsburgh had informed him that Benjamin needed to be at the hospital within six hours; otherwise, the liver would go to another child." Six hours! Dallas had not been aware of the time lost trying to locate Michael. It all seemed even more impossible.

Worst of all were the headwinds. "Think of them as a moving sidewalk," Dallas explains. "If you're walking at five miles per hour on a moving sidewalk going five miles an hour, you're really covering ten miles an hour. But if you walk in the *opposite* direction on that sidewalk, you're actually standing still." That was the effect being rendered by the headwinds. Although the plane was flying through the air at 240 knots (about 270 miles per hour), the headwinds had slowed its progress to 190 knots.

"I had a sick feeling in my stomach," Dallas says, "because I knew I had to tell the Stevermers that it was no use." They had lifted off a little after 5:00 p.m. (7:00 p.m. in Pittsburgh), and thus had less than five hours to complete a journey that, according to his calculations, would take at least seven. There was no way they could do it. Not without a miracle. Dallas put the plane on autopilot, leaned back, and closed his eyes. "Father, we need help," he prayed quietly. "This child needs to get to the hospital in time."

Almost immediately, the plane began to shake. Pilot and copilot watched the ground speed indicator in disbelief. It had started to climb. Up, up it went, from 240 to an amazing 340 knots, before the quivering stopped. The silence was broken by the voice of the Denver air traffic controller. "Lifeguard 205, you've really picked up speed. Everything okay?"

"Great!" Dallas answered, still astonished at the wind's sudden—and complete—turnaround. "We have eighty to one hundred knots right on our tail. And everything is smooth."

Pilots of larger aircraft were noticing the phenomenon, too. "What's going on?" they radioed one another. "Things are crazy tonight!" Such sudden, strong wind shifts did occur, Dallas knew, but they were extremely rare. Axnd the chance of him being in the perfect place at the exact moment when they did was even rarer.

But there were still obstacles ahead, especially the cold front expected in Chicago. When cold air slipped under the warm air, thunderstorms would result, and the little plane would lose precious time detouring around them. Now, as they approached, they could see the front, like a gray wedge lying in the star-studded sky. Yet their radar reported no storm activity. "Father," Dallas murmured again, "you're in charge, and you know what we need."

The front got closer, closer—but, unbelievably, as they approached it, it had become only a thin mist, wafting gently away into the darkness. No thunderstorms. No lengthy bypass needed after all.

The plane continued its placid journey. Just two hundred miles left until Pittsburgh. By now Dallas should have stopped for refueling. However, the unusual tailwind had pushed the plane along so fast that plenty of fuel remained. They would land at Allegheny County Airport, which was closer to the hospital, rather than the congested Pittsburgh airport, but because of this, new concerns surfaced. "The Allegheny control tower closed at midnight—it was standard procedure," Dallas says. "So there wouldn't be anyone on the ground to tell us where to park and meet the ambulance." Finding it could eat up priceless moments. And was it snowing in Pittsburgh? If visibility was limited, he would need to make a time-consuming instrument approach to the airport, or even change airport destinations.

But once again, all the decisions seemed to have been made for them. Dallas's radio crackled with an updated weather report. Pittsburgh was clear, unrestricted. There had been no snow, after all. "Oh, and by the way, Lifeguard 205," the controller casually added, "the tower is staying open until you arrive. And your ambulance is standing by at your destination."

Finally the little plane taxied to a stop and its passengers tumbled out, running toward the flickering red lights of the ambulance. "Good-bye, and thanks!" Sandi turned and waved to Dallas.

It was over. "Godspeed," he called. "We'll be praying for you."

Little Ben Stevermer received a new liver in Pittsburgh, and was home, and healthy, by Christmas. When he was two and a half, and the family had moved to the Midwest, he received an unexpected letter from Dallas Chopping. "I thought I'd wait until you were completely recovered to let you know what a special flight you were on," the letter began.

Only then did Sandi and Michael realize just what had taken place. And as Benjamin grows, they plan to tell him more about the night his heavenly Father, some Pittsburgh surgeons, and a faith-filled pilot gave him a miracle. They will explain that the plane was too small, the weather too rough, the fuel too limited—yet somehow, a seven-hour journey took only four and a half.

For nothing is impossible with God.

EPILOGUE

What you need to know about the past is that no matter what has
happened, it has all worked together to bring you to this very moment.
And this is the moment you can choose to make everything new.
Right now.

—MONICA, IN *TOUCHED BY AN ANGEL*

Sometimes it's hard to hear God's voice. Why would he speak to us, we ask? Wouldn't he rather spend his time with the wise, the saintly, and the deserving? And yet, God loves all his children. He has a plan for each of us, and he wants to be the most special part of it. "For I know well the plans I have in mind for you, says the LORD, plans for your welfare, not for woe! plans to give you a future full of hope" (Jeremiah 29:11).

What is God whispering to you? Maybe he's saying, "Come closer. Open the door of your heart to me. Try life my way, just for today."

Of course, this can be a risk. It's hard to change old attitudes, learn to forgive, honor a commitment, work for justice, bring compassion and mercy to others, and say "no" to what appears to be the easy way because we know it is not his way. Abandonment, submission, service—these are not words of the world. And yet are they not the way we change the world, one small step at a time, beginning with ourselves? Are they not the way we become his voice, his hands, his heart?

And strangely, when we let him lead, something happens. We begin to see little signs all around us, tender coincidences, good decisions magnifying like ripples on a pond, seed growing in abundance. Not always on our timetable, not always in the ways we expected, but there.

It is then that we are filled with awe at the wonder of it all, at the doors that are opening to our knock, the marvels we shall seek and find because we have decided, at last, to say "Yes!"

It is then that we glimpse heaven and understand its everlasting truth, that in this world of change and darkness, we have nothing to fear. He has been there all along. And his light is eternal. His love prevails.

NOTES

1. Roberts Liardon, *I Saw Heaven* (Tulsa, OK: Harrison House, 1983), 17.

2. Rex Hauck, ed., *Angels: The Mysterious Messengers* (New York: Ballantine Books, 1994), 97.

3. *In the Company of Angels*, VHS (Harrison, NY: Ignatius Press, 1995).

4. This story was first documented by Arvin S. Gibson for inclusion in his book *Glimpses of Eternity* (Bountiful, UT: Horizon, 1992). According to him, Ann is now an adult and prefers to remain anonymous. Her leukemia has never returned.

5. Lew Baker is the founder of Open Hands Prison Ministries, a ministry for alcoholic prison inmates. For more information, contact him at PO Box 201, Pine Valley, NY, 14872.

6. Pythia Peay, "Heaven Sent," *Washingtonian*, December 1993, 90.

7. Mickey Robinson's lectures help people reach their personal potential and find their own gifts and talents. For information on his lectures or his book, *Falling to Heaven*, contact him at

Prophetic Destiny International, PO Box 682485, Franklin, TN, 37068, 615-595-0653.

BIBLIOGRAPHY AND RESOURCES

Nonfiction

Callanan, Maggie, and Patricia Kelley. *Final Gifts: Understanding the Special Awareness, Needs, and Communications of the Dying.* New York: Poseidon Press, 1992.

Brown, Michael H. *The Trumpet of Gabriel.* Milford, OH: Faith Publishing Company, 1994.

————. *The Final Hour.* Milford, OH: Faith Publishing Company, 1992.

Dossey, Larry. *Healing Words: The Power of Prayer and the Practice of Medicine.* San Francisco: HarperSanFrancisco, 1993.

Finley, Mitch. *Whispers of Love: Encounters with Deceased Relatives and Friends.* New York: Crossroad Publishing, 1995.

Fullman, Lynn Grisard. *Alabama Miracles: Real Life Stories to Warm the Heart.* Birmingham, AL: Seacoast Publishing, Inc., 1994.

Groeschel, Benedict J., CFR. *A Still, Small Voice: A Practical Guide on Reported Revelations.* San Francisco: Ignatius Press, 1993.

Kreeft, Peter J. *Angels and Demons: What Do We Really Know about Them?* San Francisco: Ignatius Press, 1995.

Lewis, C. S. *Miracles.* New York: Macmillan, 1947.

Morse, Melvin, MD, with Paul Perry. *Parting Visions: Uses and Meanings of Pre-death, Psychic, and Spiritual Experiences.* New York: Villard Books, 1994.

Sanford, John A. *Dreams: God's Forgotten Language.* Philadelphia and New York: J. B. Lippincott Company, 1968.

Schlink, M. Basilea. *Nature Out of Control?* Harpenden, Herts, England: Kanaan Publications, 1994.

Spangler, Ann. *An Angel a Day: Stories of Angelic Encounters.* Grand Rapids, MI: Zondervan Publishing House, 1994.

Fiction

Pochocki, Ethel. *The Wind Harp and Other Angel Tales.* Cincinnati, OH: St. Anthony Messenger Press, 1995.

Videos

The Greatest Miracles on Earth, DVD. The Entertainment Group, 4570 NE Indian River Drive, Jenson Beach, FL, 877-337-2100.

Publications

Angels on Earth. Guideposts, PO Box 856, Carmel, NY, 10512; bimonthly publication.

Organizations

Angel Collectors Club of America (ACCA). Paulette Konopka, PO Box 824, Ocean Gate, NJ, 08740. New membership dues $20.00 per year.

Angels of the World International (AWI). Suzanne Vecchiarelli, 8 Bellwood Drive, New City, NY, 10955. Membership dues $10.00 per year.

International Association of Near-Death Studies (IANDS). 2741 Campus Walk Avenue, Building 500, Durham, NC 27705-8878, http://www .iands.org. New membership dues $30.00 per year.

Author's Afterword

I am always interested in hearing from readers who would like to share their angel encounters, miracles, answers to prayer, and other heavenly wonders. Please write to me at PO Box 127, Prospect Heights, IL 60070, or visit my Web site at http:/www.joanwanderson .com.

If I can use your story in my future writing, I will contact you for permission.

Joan Wester Anderson
joan@joanwanderson.com

ABOUT THE AUTHOR

Joan Wester Anderson is the best-selling author of *Where Angels Walk, Where Miracles Happen*, and *An Angel to Watch Over Me*. Her work, totaling sixteen books and more than a thousand articles and stories, has also been published in newspapers and in such magazines as *Reader's Digest, Modern Bride*, and *Woman's Day*. The author has appeared on *Oprah, Good Morning America, NBC Nightly News*, and many other national and local shows. She and her husband live in a Chicago suburb. They have five grown children and four grandchildren.

Also available by Joan Wester Anderson

The Power of Miracles
True Stories of God's Presence

Paperback • 256 pages • ISBN: 978-0-8294-2213-9 • $14.95

In the Arms of Angels
True Stories of Heavenly Guardians

Paperback • 296 pages • ISBN: 978-0-8294-2040-1 • $14.95

Guardian Angels
True Stories of Answered Prayers

Paperback • 240 pages • ISBN: 978-0-8294-2169-9 • $14.95

LOYOLAPRESS.
A JESUIT MINISTRY

Phone: 800-621-1008   Fax: 773-281-0555   Visit: www.loyolapress.com